MDSOC.∅

POST-INDUSTRIAL
CAPITALISM

POST-INDUSTRIAL CAPITALISM

EXPLORING ECONOMIC INEQUALITY IN AMERICA

JOEL I. NELSON

SAGE Publications
International Educational and Professional Publisher
Thousand Oaks   London   New Delhi

For information address:

 SAGE Publications, Inc*:*
2455 Teller Road
Thousand Oaks, California 91320
E-mail: order@sagepub.com

SAGE Publications Ltd.
6 Bonhill Street
London EC2A 4PU
United Kingdom

SAGE Publications India Pvt. Ltd.
M-32 Market
Greater Kailash I
New Delhi 110 048 India

Printed in the United States of America

Library of Congress Cataloging-in-Publication Data

Nelson, Joel I.
   Post-industrial capitalism: Exploring economic inequality in America / Joel I. Nelson.
      p.   cm.
   Includes bibliographical references and index.
   ISBN 0-8039-7332-2 (alk. paper).—ISBN 0-8039-7333-0 (pbk.: alk. paper)
   1. United States—Economic conditions—1981- 2. Capitalism—United States. 3. Income distribution—United States. 4. Poverty—United States. 5. Wealth—United States. I. Title.
HC106.8.N453   1995
330.973—dc20   95-8957

This book is printed on acid-free paper.

95 96 97 98 99 10 9 8 7 6 5 4 3 2 1

Sage Production Editor: Diana E. Axelsen
Sage Typesetter: Andrea D. Swanson

Contents

Post-Industrial Capitalism

Progress is everywhere uneven. Women continue to be disadvantaged. Minorities remain oppressed. Inequities persist. Yet, compared to the past several centuries—to the agrarian empires and feudal kingdoms of a former age—the economies of most advanced industrialized nations today are vastly more equitable and just. Material well-being has increased. Health and comfort have advanced. Longevity has been extended. Industrial capitalism has improved standards of living, diminished inequality, and introduced a broad menu of security programs associated with the welfare state. There is no question of this: Most people in advanced economies are better off today than their ancestors of a century or more ago.

But substantial evidence suggests that economic progress, at least in the United States, is increasingly blocked. In the past decade or two, the social and economic well-being of many Americans has been in jeopardy. Many Americans have no clear sense of a better future. Excesses of the free market are growing, and growing more difficult to contain. The signs are everywhere: in dismal ghettos, in rising disparities in earnings and wealth, in disregard for disadvantaged minorities and the homeless, in the declining employment options of once powerful corporations, in the increasing tolerance for unemployment (over inflation), in the conviction across the ideological

spectrum that competitiveness and economic vitality are more important than assistance and humanitarian aid.

The resurgence of free market ideology is at the root of recent
growth in inequality. This resurgence, according to John Goldthorpe
(1984), is the new laissez faire: the concern with market freedom in
the context of a welfare state. At the same time, markets show
renewed vigor: in blatant financial manipulation, in antagonism
toward organized labor, and in a partial dismantling of welfare
programs amid pockets of poverty. Markets are contained, Karl
Polanyi (1957) has written, because of the misery they create. But
recent events suggest a triumph of the free market.

No shortage of explanations exists. Interpretations of inequality
and a resurgence of the free market are everywhere. In this volume
on post-industrial capitalism, I consider rising inequality in American society—but with a different twist. My argument looks not to
any crisis in capitalism but to the new vigor and resources—to the
Schumpeterian concept of creative energy—that *activates* the corporate quest for profits (Schumpeter 1934). The centerpiece of my
position is that in recent years corporations have acquired new
resources, qualitatively different from those available in the past.
These resources are organizational and knowledge-based and are
tantamount to a revolution in the inventory of tactics and strategies
available to corporations. In this volume, I describe the shifts in
corporate resources, illustrate their use by the corporate sector, and
trace their implications for inequality across different sectors of the
institutional spectrum. I will show how corporations have used these
strategies to intensify competition, affect greater political control,
and widen the gap between rich and poor in America today.

In emphasizing changing corporate resources, I underline the new
opportunities businesses pursue—rather than the constraints, the
obstacles, and missed opportunities more commonly emphasized in
other discussions of inequality. The media, for example, provide a
daily dose of stories about inequality and the resurgent market. For
the most part, the growing importance of the market is defined in
terms of the country's economic ills. These ills are diagnosed as
effects of a bewildering array of events, including the climate and
excesses of the 1980s, OSHA, deindustrialization, short-sighted corporate leadership, failing productivity, reversals in union strength,
Ronald Reagan, George Bush, the service society, a declining work
ethic, cyclical politics, cheap labor in the underdeveloped world, and

the emerging preeminence of Japan and the "four little dragons" along the Pacific rim.

These popular explanations convey only fragments of a changing America. Many are either suspect, incorrect, or based on faulty premises. They refer to short-term and specific events, singling out one or another historical circumstance. Causes are separated, obscuring possible insight into major structural shifts throughout the economic order. Explanations allude to the problems of America, ignoring similar difficulties faced by most of the economically advanced nations of the world—including rising inequality (Davis 1992). Most of all, these explanations incorrectly portray business as victim: of tough international competitors, of indifferent workers, of corporate managers forsaking American prosperity for short-term gain and paper profits. They ignore the vitality of business as illustrated in the escalating proportion of managers and professionals, the proliferating numbers of business schools, and the increasing predominance of MBAs. They ignore, in brief, the very spirit of the business enterprise itself.

Classical social theory is not more helpful than the media. It likewise offers scant insight into growing inequality. Several decades ago, post-industrial theorists speculated on the far-reaching possibilities of endless innovations in knowledge and technology (Bell 1973). Rising affluence and increased productivity would abolish poverty. Marxist-oriented theorists, ever at the vigil for signs of the growing concentration of capital, were more sensitive to the market's resurgence (Bluestone and Harrison 1982). But the hope of Marxists, in the form of class-conscious workers, has not emerged to constrain a resurgent market. These two theories, central as they are to stratification, ignore the decision making and expertise captured in the vision of capitalism building on and creatively destroying its past. They consequently miss how dramatic and recent innovations in business are central both to the renaissance of the market and to recent escalation in economic inequality.

THE CASE FOR POST-INDUSTRIAL CAPITALISM: A BRIEF INTRODUCTION

Capitalism is about the pursuit of profit. Capitalism flourishes under varying opportunity structures, each providing new alternatives for profit and new alternatives for social control. Under industrial capitalism, opportunities and resources primarily advanced techniques in production. Machines and machine efficiency were the bywords of commerce and industry. In the past, economic development fed social development. For many, social and economic development formed a singular and seamless thread. The productivity of core industrial corporations was connected to the economic and political interests of a stable and skilled workforce. The connection forged a link between growth and equity. But now the link between growth and equality has been severed.

American society is on the precipice of a new era in the development of capitalism—an era of post-industrial capitalism. The changes associated with this era are largely responsible for increasing inequality and breaking the Gordian knot linking growth to inequality. Under post-industrial capitalism, businesses use new resources to supplement the engineering and production skills identified with the rapid industrialization of the past. The newer resources generate alternative strategies and organizational alliances that increase the ability of business to handle complex markets. By increasing the scope and intensity of competition and by heightening political control, these practices, in effect, undermine the sources of equality present in the era of industrial capitalism: the high profits and high wages in the monopoly sector, the more minor growth in peripheral industries, the strong unions, as well as the expanding welfare state.

Under post-industrial capitalism, new resources are identified with across-the-board innovations in strategy, including inventory control, market analysis, product testing, cash budgeting, portfolio analysis, financial and cost control, accounting, capital investment analysis, advertising, public relations, strategic planning, research, technological forecasting, product innovation, management consulting services, political advising, and issue management. These resources reflect the escalating knowledge base of capitalism. My reference to and definition of knowledge here is quite specific: an organized and objective interpretation of information. This knowledge base develops in tandem with rising levels of education and expanding literacy of a more professional and specialized white-collar workforce.

Post-industrial capitalism is fueled by the continuing impact of the managerial revolution: in the increased control of management, in the professionalization of managerial functions, and in a more varied corporate structure—more loosely federated, more professional, and less rule-bound than in the past. Popular and technical texts applaud the merits of the managerial revolution. They laud the virtuosity of managerial capitalism, the victory of organizational acumen over market forces. They draw on the criteria of neoclassical economics. What is efficient is best.

At the same time, all these writings fail to note a darker side to this vision of growth in managerial strategies: a sharpening of inequality and a renaissance of market forces accompanying the growth in business knowledge and managerial functions. The goal of the so-called managerial revolution has been to enlarge economic competition. There is reason to believe that this goal has been accomplished. But scholars continue to ignore the social costs of inequality resulting from this revolution. They ignore the role of competition in driving down the wages of labor, the variable costs of production. It is as if business transactions do not involve workers and as if the costs of competition are to corporations without regard to labor at all.

Post-industrial capitalism addresses the influence of proliferating administrative technologies on inequality in two institutional domains—in the economic and the political institutions. Although these domains are different, each illustrates how inequality and competition escalate as barriers to the diffusion of information break down and ever more flexible (and more competitive) organizational forms arise. In the economic area, for example, structural processes are put in place—in the form of corporate departments and full-time staffs—to persistently explore competitive strategies and to systematically scan the competition with a view toward honing a sharper competitive edge. Not surprisingly, wages and declining labor costs spearhead competition.

In the political sphere, similar processes are in place. Large corporations use knowledge and information to increase control and to exploit political and economic circumstances. These resources draw on sundry organizational forms to accommodate quality circles, technically sophisticated lobbyists, election campaign consultants, pollsters, advertisers, public relations firms, focus groups, media specialists, and others expert in controlling information and managing conflict. These resources do not guarantee omnipotence, but they contribute to a rapidly deteriorating labor movement and to fragmentation in a coalition for the working class. These resources also reinforce an increasingly symbiotic alliance of business and government. They undermine the unions, the welfare net, the working-class coalitions responsible for effecting equality in previous times.

Effective political control suggests, however, that there is more to recent inequality than meets the eye. In traditional social theory, escalating inequality provoked social conflict. Conflict galvanized support to arrest class polarization. Under post-industrial capitalism, inequality increases in the absence of conflict—without a strong union movement, without a stable left-of-center political organization, and, more generally, in the context of political tranquility. Thus the paradox of post-industrial capitalism: liberal apathy in a core of mounting inequality.

The theory of post-industrial capitalism thus links the resurgence of inequality and free market ideology to the transformation of American business. The theory concurs with post-industrial theorists: Knowledge is expanding and is the key resource in the modern world. But this is not knowledge for its own sake. It is knowledge in service of the corporation—a point post-industrial theorists generally ignored. Although the promise of the expansion in knowledge is a more rational, efficient, and productive business enterprise, the most immediate effect is to sharpen inequality. Knowledge and organizational resources provide an edge in putting together a world more attentive to competition and corporate profits than to the needs of ordinary workers. This edge, reflected in the dramatic escalation of economic inequality in the absence of conflict, leads to the unsettling conclusion of growing inequality as a new and permanent feature in American society—with effects present long after the excesses of the 1980s or the Carter, Bush, and Reagan administrations recede into memory.

AMERICAN CLASS STRUCTURE: THE WIDENING GAP

Every generation thinks of itself as novel or unique, a watershed in history. But it is risky intellectual business to divide history into distinctive epochs. I begin my argument by considering recent trends in stratification and inequality and by illustrating how these trends are not easily explained by existing theory. I must emphasize that although I discuss other forms of inequality, my chief concern in this volume is the increasing disparities in income and wealth. In this, I agree with Nielsen's (1994, p. 674) contention that increasing inequality in economically advanced societies should be prominent "on the agenda of stratification research."

I will argue that understanding trends in inequality is best served by the theory and concept of post-industrial capitalism. The following points of departure are simple but central to this argument:

- Inequality has increased dramatically in recent years—intensifying American stratification.
- This increase represents a radical and discontinuous shift of trends in inequality.
- Discontinuous shifts in inequality reflect major transformations, new stages, in the American economy.

Although other arguments consider recent growth in inequality, most look backward into the past: denying the permanence of major structural changes; drawing primarily on the major concepts of industrial capitalism—capital intensiveness, productivity, and scale; alluding to a flawed system precipitating America's fall from industrial primacy to an economic power of the second rank.

Industrialization and Inequality

Not all will agree with estimates of declining disparities in the American class structure. But this, nonetheless, is what the legacy of theory and empirical work suggests: declining inequality as industrialization advances. The theory implied is straightforward. Agrarian societies are unequal because of the enormous disparity between rich and poor. As industrialization proceeds, ordinary workers gain— moving median income to a point where disparities attenuate between the rich and the average worker. Hence equality increases as the economic pie expands. In comparison with nonmechanized agriculture, capital-intensive manufacturing increases productivity, hence stimulating sales and profits. Higher wage demands, fostered by unionization, are applied against greater profits, allowing all parties to benefit simultaneously from the growth spurred by industrialization (Lenski 1966; Williamson and Lindert 1980).

This idealized version of the relationship of industrialization to equality has been partially supported by data on historical trends in the American class structure. Soltow's (1971, pp. 318-19) exacting study of historical trends in urban Wisconsin concluded that inequality declined over approximately a century's time: "The strongly urban area of Milwaukee County had an inequality coefficient of income somewhere between 0.55 and 0.75 in 1864. The coefficient was 0.35 in 1959." Although Wisconsin is only one state, Soltow's conclusions are similar to estimates from other countries, indicating growth in equality with advancing industrialization (Kuznets 1955;

Nielsen 1994; Peters 1973; Soltow 1965, 1968). They also are consistent with alternative estimates of declines in American earnings inequality. Williamson and Lindert (1980), for example, also see declining inequality during the period of intense industrialization, from about 1900 to 1950, although in their view, this decline was not quite as apparent prior to 1900.

As to wealth, problems abound in comparing estimates over a 100-year time span. Nonetheless, the evidence on wealth indicates declines in inequality as a function of advancing industrialization—although the evidence is generally more complex and more ambiguous than it is with earnings. Several studies indicate that wealth inequality is unrelated to early industrialization. Soltow (1975), for example, argued that wealth inequality was more or less stable from the middle of the 19th century up through the Depression. Other estimates suggest inequality during the same time period may actually have increased (*New York Times* 1992e).

There is more consensus, however, that in late industrialization—with escalating uses in electricity and petroleum fuel for manufacturing—productivity is sufficiently high to increase the wealth of ordinary workers and consequently diminish overall inequality. Smith (1984), for example, extended earlier estimates of inequality (given by Lampman 1962) that suggest sharp declines from 1920 to the mid-1970s. In their estimate, the top one-half of one percent of the wealthiest individuals controlled 30% of the wealth in the early 1920s, compared to 14% about 50 years later. Wolff and Marley (1989) show identical estimates for individuals and parallel estimates for households duri.·g the same period. If pensions are included in defining wealth, the decline for the period is steep and precipitous (Wolff and Marley 1989). These estimates closely resemble other estimates for Great Britain (Shorrocks 1987) and for Sweden (Spant 1987).

Recent Trends in Economic Inequality

Recent events, however, have reversed trends in declining inequality. In the last decade or so, inequality has increased dramatically, altering previous American experience. Details splashed across magazine and newspaper headlines herald a decline in the middle class. The distance between the top and the bottom has increased rather than diminished. Using data from two surveys of consumer finances, Wolff (1992) estimated that the top 1% of the wealthiest households increased their control of total wealth from 19% in 1976 to 24% in 1981. Using different materials, a recent report by the Federal Reserve and the Internal Revenue Service indicated that the richest 1% of American households increased their net worth from 31% of total wealth in 1983 to 37% in 1989 (*New York Times* 1992a).

Statistics on income show similar trends. An important study by Maxwell (1989) reported a steady erosion of income shares by the poorest 40% of earners from 1960 to 1980. In 1960, the bottom two quintiles earned 13% of total income, compared to 9% in 1980. Comparable material from the census indicates similar trends. The share of money income of the bottom two fifths of American families over the last decade has declined, whereas the share of the top fifth has increased. From 1980 to 1987, aggregate income controlled by the poorest two fifths of families in America decreased from 16.7% to 15.4% while the wealthiest one fifth increased from 41.6% to 43.7% (U.S. Bureau of the Census 1990a, p. 451). This is an enormous change in a short period of time. The change, however, reflects the gradual increase in inequality over the last several decades, from approximately the mid-1960s to the present (Maxwell 1989). Citing a report by the Congressional Budget Office, the *New York Times* (1992b) noted that 1% of the richest American families reaped most of the benefits of prosperity over the last 15 to 20 years.

Most analysts concur on the recent growth in inequality—and the sharp turn in experience from the past. These facts are not in dispute. But analysts do not agree on what these events mean. Nor do they agree on how they are to be explained. Consider, for example, the charge that recent changes in inequality increase because of growth in demography, public policy, or the cycles of economic growth and recession—rather than any fundamental shifts in economic structure. In a widely read (and well-reviewed) study on inequality in America, economist Frank Levy (1988, p. 197) explains growth in inequality as follows:

> Much of the growing inequality was due to the continued increase in female-headed families, a trend which redefined the nature of the lowest quintile. But after 1979, inequality was reinforced by the deep recession and declining means-tested benefits, both of which undermined the lowest quintiles.

These statements provide ammunition to advance policies aimed at reducing welfare benefits for single women with children. The purpose of these policies is to eliminate poverty. But ignored are some stark facts about poverty in America today—among them the fact that people have less money today because they earn less money. A recent U.S. census report (*New York Times* 1992c) indicated a 50% increase in low-paying jobs during the 1980s. The working poor are a new and significant presence in American society. They number nearly 1 in every 5 workers. Furthermore, poverty is not the province of single mothers. Poverty increased among all families, not merely among single mothers. And government policies, such as they are, to cope with poverty are widely ineffective (Cutler and Katz 1992). Ignored likewise in Levy's assertions is the fact that poverty rates are tied neither to economic growth nor recession—as they have been in the past. Inequality rose in the 1980s, even though economic growth was not significantly slower than in the post-World War II boom of the 1950s (U.S. Bureau of the Census 1991, p. 427). The benefits of recent growth, however, did not trickle down to the poor; they were more likely found in the lush suburban and silk stocking districts of the American metropolis than in neighborhoods of the inner city. Comparing two periods of substantial and comparable growth, 1963-1969 with 1983-1989, Rebecca Blank (1991) concluded that growth no longer erodes poverty. This is a fundamental change in the American economy. In the 1960s, growth in the gross national product (GNP) was associated with declining poverty, but this was not true in the 1980s. Blank concluded that the prosperity of the 1980s had little influence on poverty and furthermore that economic growth is no longer a painless way to cure poverty.

In brief, evidence suggests a changing character to the recent and unprecedented escalation in inequality. The evidence also suggests significant changes in America—with inequality an important barometer of shifts in the economy, in politics, and in social life. These shifts are scattered across the American landscape in severe cutbacks in welfare, in downsizing corporations, in the decline of unions, and in rising tolerance for higher unemployment. Much ink has been spent on explaining these changes. Although I will deal with many of these explanations in other chapters, I must single out several general themes here and the presuppositions on which they rest. In various ways, each illustrates the same recalcitrance, an unwillingness to admit that anything is new under the sun. In various ways, each looks backward, searching past formulas for explaining a qualitatively changing future. Each raises the wrong questions—generating little more than wrong answers.

Looking Backward

Many explanations of inequality assume a golden era in America's past—a time of abundance after World War II when workers were affluent, the economy productive, and the nation hegemonic in the world order. In this past, American manufacturing accounted for fully one half of world production. Today, that contribution to world production is embarrassingly less. The reasons given for this decline vary from detailed considerations of particular events to damning condemnations of recent business practices. Alfred Chandler (1990), for example, discusses American decline in terms of industrial expansion without the core skills required for competitive advantage. Edward Luttwak (1994, p. 48) considers the recurrent theme of falling productivity, noting that America's superiority in productivity has been reduced by more than 50%. Other theorists go further in suggesting that management continues to relegate American business to the garbage heap of failed capitalist enterprises (Minsky 1986; Reich 1984). Corporations, in this view, are not engines for growth but invitations for disaster—as reflected in the financial excesses of Wall Street and the failure of American business to invest in research and development and needed capital equipment. The same pursuit of short-term gain is the core of Bluestone and Harrison's (1982) indictment of managers exporting high-wage manufacturing jobs elsewhere, leaving American workers in competition with cheap labor abroad or dismissed to dead-end jobs behind the golden arches.

These views all converge on a similar theme of a flawed economy with mistakes in investments and production. Flaw leads to blame, and blame is laid on career managers or the stockholders behind them, pushing for profits, even paper profits, at any and all costs (Useem 1993). But are these assertions realistic? Should explanations be framed in terms of a flawed economy deviating from an idealized past when things worked well or better? By framing economic problems only in terms of American experience, these views ignore worldwide growth in inequality and economic problems (Davis 1992). An analysis of "American decline" cannot furnish useful answers to problems common to the industrial world. Furthermore, the inference of these analyses seems to be that, were these flaws absent, the trajectory of America simply and persistently would be global hegemony—now and forever.

The question of accounting for America's recent decline belies a still more vital and important question: Has America declined? The base point for measuring decline is usually immediately after World War II, a unique historical period when America's fiercest competitors were much involved in the aftermath of the devastating effects of combat and warfare (Nye 1990). The fact is that today the United States produces about the same share of the world's output as it did immediately prior to World War I. And in 1938, industrial output per capita was barely ahead of output in Britain, Germany, and Sweden (Bairoch 1982).

Many discussions of national decline portray America as a former industrial giant—suggesting that industry and hard work were common characteristics of a bygone era. Ignored is the possibility that happenstance and circumstance (rather than hard work and industrial savvy) shaped American destiny. Yet, as Gavin Wright (1990, pp. 656-57) has shown, the country's rise to industrial power "was not marked by a shift towards capital-intensive manufacturing exports, nor by an increasing tendency to trade capital-intensive for labor-intensive manufactures with the rest of the world." Rather, processed natural resources dominated American industry, providing the basis for world economic power. In conclusion, Wright (1990, p. 665) insightfully remarks on the unwillingness of most Americans to "attribute their country's industrial success to what appear to be accidental or fortuitous geographic circumstances."

The vision of a golden past persists. Alan Blinder (*Business Week* 1992a, p. 16) has remarked that "Americans are haunted by the memory of the 1950s"—what he cynically labels the "Ozzie and Harriet" years. The economic preeminence of America during the 1950s is simply an historical artifact. To use the decline in American fortunes to explain current trends in economic inequality is to offer a problematic answer to the wrong question. Other alternatives are available for explaining economic change—without casting blame or seeing the economy as a flawed or moribund enterprise.

KNOWLEDGE AND INEQUALITY: THE NEW FOUNDATIONS OF CONTEMPORARY CAPITALISM

Profits fuel capitalism. But how and where profits are attained, the inequalities they produce, and the forces likely to rise in opposition to inequality—these are partially shaped by technological regimes. Technological regimes are clusters of new resources, offering novel opportunities for economic development. These resources influence the directions businesses take and their responses to new circumstances. In this view, the business of business is the search for profits, but the conduit for profits is ever changing. Resources and regimes condition the opportunities and the search for alternative sources of profit.

Capitalism flourishes under a variety of industrial regimes—agriculture, commerce, or manufacturing. Each regime allows capitalism to develop differently, to seize different opportunities for profits, control, and political alliance (Stinchcombe 1961). The history of capitalism charts how innovations in technology—in transportation, in factories and factory organization, in the industrial uses of electricity, energy, and combustion—provide opportunities to enhance profits. Each innovation crosses a different barrier, a different constraint in the search for profits. Each alters the way capitalism works. These technological developments inform the institutional codes and rules of capitalism, the blueprints, indicating where profits may be attained and how they are to be sought.

In the recent past, the production costs of goods largely determined the range of opportunities for profit. Today managerial strategies increasingly supplement production costs as a determinant of corporate profits. These strategies are informational and organizational. They are highly flexible means to acquire, store, and modify information related to profits, to business contingencies, and to economic trends. Managerial strategies, of course, always existed. But the rising specialization in services, particularly in managerial and consultant services, provides a qualitatively new base of resources and knowledge for enhancing profit. These changes reflect new and innovative tools in business and represent a basic shift in how businesses conduct their affairs. They suggest new alternatives for businesses to pursue. Because of problems in information or organization, these alternatives either were not pursued in the past or were pursued inadequately.

The shifting resources of business affect the many factors related to social stratification and inequality: the internationalization of markets and the ascendence of new economic firms, as well as changes in unions, politics, and welfare. These resources influence inequality in two ways:

1. They qualitatively enlarge the scope and intensity of economic competition, pressing wages downward to affect greater productivity.

2. They more effectively neutralize the politics of adversaries.

In this way, inequality increases, not because of a flawed economy but as an outgrowth of the rationalization of resources—a process with deep roots in capitalist development.

The exponential growth in these resources—in business knowledge and business rationality—characterizes a new era in the way firms and corporations go about acquiring profits. I refer to this as an era of *post-industrial capitalism*. Capitalism, of course, always revolves around markets, and markets, as Alan Wolfe (1989, p. 77) has argued, are always there, a constant in social affairs. But the rules and constraints governing market activity change over time. Under post-industrial capitalism, markets are freer and more influential. They are more likely to be shaped by managerial strategy and less likely to be constrained by intervention from political elites.

The selection of the term *post-industrial capitalism* is intended to contrast the effects of capitalism today with its effects in an industrial past. Post-industrial capitalism illustrates what Hannan and Freeman (1989, p. 54) refer to as "blending" processes, reflecting how innovations in organizational structure and managerial strategy increasingly blend into and supplement innovations in productive technology. As noted previously, post-industrial capitalism involves shifting corporate resources. But post-industrial capitalism does not involve any shift in the fundamental processes of capitalism, as reflected in the competitive search for economic advantage or political dominance.

What this new and blended form of capitalism does, however, is produce a transformation, a qualitative and discontinuous shift in class structure. That is, the contrast of past and present is indicated not merely by the blended form capitalism assumes but also by its influence on inequality. In a previous time, economic development fed social development by diminishing inequality; today, economic development escalates inequality. In this sense, the altered resources associated with post-industrial capitalism result in a new principle of economic growth. This section discusses two issues related to these resources: first, what these resources are—leaving to later chapters the discussion of how they work; second, an initial summary about the influence of these resources on politics and the economy, illustrating how and why post-industrial capitalism increases inequality in the American class structure.

Inequality and the Managerial Revolution

To account for recent developments and newer foundations for inequality, numerous scholars have suggested that capitalism be divided into time periods. These foundations are more precise than the Marxist legacy of feudalism, capitalism, and socialism. Post-industrial capitalism summarizes many of these distinctions. Heydebrand (1983, 1989) and Wright and Martin (1987), for example, recommend joining the analysis of capitalism to post-industrial theory—dividing capitalism into industrial and post-industrial periods (see also Jameson 1971 and Mandel 1976). Burawoy (1979) refers to a new era of market expansion, an era less generous to and protective of workers. Castells (1976) connects the emerging service economy to recent crises within capitalism. Lash and Urry (1987) distinguish between organized and disorganized capitalism, with disorganized capitalism fragmenting and decentralizing the connections between workers, core manufacturers, unions, and the state.

Mainstream writings on organizational change also point to recent and important alterations in industrial economies—and to qualitative shifts in capitalism. Notable here are writings on the transformation of capitalism from roots in family structure to control by managers and professionals. Early on, James Burnham (1941) coined the concept of a managerial revolution and referred to a transfer of power to a broad stratum of middle-class managers. Numerous other writers likewise commented on the demise of family capitalism and the transfer of power to managerial hands—ushering in an epoch of *managerial capitalism* (Bell 1962; Berle and Means 1932; Useem 1990). These writers all concur on the recent importance of managerial strategies in the conduct of modern business firms. In *The Visible Hand,* Chandler (1977) highlights the managerial revolution by showing how market forces succumbed to managerial strategy. John Kenneth Galbraith (1967) also emphasizes the role of technocrats in managing and directing the economic order. All of these writings discuss the course and direction of capitalism in affecting greater corporate control over the marketplace.

The same concern with managers and managerial strategy—and the same implication of mastery over the market—is the text for recent and popular writings on business analysis. I refer to Porter's (1985, 1988) works on competitive strategy, as well as to numerous best-selling managerial primers: Peters and Waterman's (1982) *In*

Search of Excellence, Leavitt's (1986) *The Marketing Imagination*, and Kanter's (1983) *The Change Masters*. Although the particulars of these works are diverse, all celebrate new corporate forms, more innovative and less constrained by rules and traditions. All point to an emergent corporation transcending the monolithic industrial bureaucracy of the past.

The theory of post-industrial capitalism draws on many of these ideas and distinctions, particularly on the key concept of a managerial revolution. But my concern is less in the shifts and contrasting interests of family and managers and more in the increasingly rationalized criteria and resources used in decisions. That is, rather than focus on the structural interests of family and kin, I find it more useful to go directly to the heart of the matter: the criteria used for making decisions and the resources used to implement them. Specifically, how do managers—whether professionals, technocrats, family owners, or some combination of these—make decisions? What resources do they draw on? What decisions do they make?

I also take issue with the temporal dimensions implied by the managerial revolution. The managerial revolution signifies a quick and sudden transformation of capital and control, a "big bang" view of social change. But much social change, including the so-called "industrial revolution," is discontinuous and gradual. Deane (1965), for example, points out that late into the 19th century, wooden machines were still prevalent throughout much of Great Britain. Likewise, with the managerial revolution. Although many of the largest corporations were administered by professional managers early on (Herman 1981), the managerial revolution, like a scientific paradigm, is continually explored, reexplored, and reworked. Witness, for example, the recent transformation of retail trade and personal services from a virtual "mom-and-pop" store industry to a world of chain stores, megamalls, and corporate-based specialty outlets. To pinpoint the managerial revolution as a specific event, dated in time with a specific beginning and a definite ending, ignores the continuous ramifications of change and its novel appearance in new institutional contexts.

I take issue with the writing on the managerial revolution in another way as well. The concept of a managerial revolution links organizational change to the firm's ability to overcome complexity and uncertainty. The concept emphasizes the growth of efficiency in organization and production. But these views depict organizational change in a vacuum. In this vacuum, capitalism is analyzed from the distinctly singular perspective of elites, unconcerned by the problems of workers, wages, and inequality. The efficiencies implied by classical economics are highlighted. Marx, however, is ignored.

Nearly all writing on the managerial revolution consequently fails to note another side to the market triumphant: the increased disparities in income and wealth accompanying the ascendance of the managerial function. The aim of managerial strategy is to achieve competitive advantage. To the extent that this occurs throughout the market, only a small step is necessary, following Marx, to suggest additional consequences: pressure to decrease costs—in which labor is a chief target. As wages decline, as poor-paying jobs increase, as middle-income workers increasingly experience deteriorating economic fortunes, inequality spirals. In brief, inequality and the managerial strategies implied in post-industrial capitalism go together. This connection between inequality and the changing organization of business is the core of my argument.

In exploring change in the management of firms, I focus on rapid growth in knowledge-based business resources. Several decades ago, Bell (1973) predicted an emergent post-industrial society with knowledge as an essential ingredient. He portrayed knowledge as a collective resource, a free-floating commodity managed by professionals in a new era of social development. Knowledge, in Bell's view, altered the course of capitalism and changed its essential characteristics (Harrington 1976). But knowledge, as I formerly suggested, is the dependent factor, the condition—developed and put to use by particular groups for particular purposes. Consequently, the impact of knowledge is dependent on the elites who mobilize it for their own structural interests and ulterior ends. Post-industrial theorists failed to ask and answer the questions of knowledge for what? knowledge for whom? I pose this question and provide an answer with a different angle of vision: knowledge advanced to further the interests of the corporation.

The Dimensions of Post-Industrial Capitalism

In past writings, rationality and innovation are discussed primarily in terms of the technical efficiency of production (Elster 1983; Nelson and Winter 1982). But innovation and rationality are also about the logic in arranging managerial structure to optimize corporate goals—most notably sales and profits. Following Erik Wright's (Wright 1985; Wright and Martin 1987) important lead in revising Marxist conceptions of resources, I see three factors involved in rationalizing managerial practices. These factors shape the cultural framework that structures rationalization, indicating how knowledge is applied to business and the conduct of the corporation and most important, suggesting what is at stake in the altered structure of capitalism. The three factors involve the following:

> an expanding domain of managerial activity,
> an enlarged foundation of business knowledge, and
> an altered organization to facilitate the use of strategy for competitive advantage.

Again I must emphasize that my interest in the managerial revolution is less in the separation of family and capitalism and more in decision making and strategy: the content of these decisions, the resources used to formulate them, and the organizational contexts in which they are developed. As a prelude to considering the influence of competition on inequality, I briefly review some of these ideas. The ideas simply summarize what has been discussed extensively elsewhere: the ABCs of managerial thinking outlined in the works of Drucker (1964, 1974), Porter (1985, 1988), Ansoff (1965), and other strategic management theorists (Oster 1990; Miller 1986).

  1. *Resources Under Post-Industrial Capitalism: The Expanding Domain of Activity.* The managerial revolution is predicated on a domain of corporate activity more broadly defined than production and social control. This domain expanded in tandem with the explosive growth in the social sciences—most notably in economics, sociology, psychology, and organizational theory. Several distinctions sort the multiple and interrelated arenas of economic activity relevant to managerial activities, including the familiar categories of manufacturing and services. Here I use Parsons's (1960) distinction between three levels of organizational concern: the technical, managerial, and institutional.

  The technical system, the first category in Parsons's analysis, refers to the actual production of basic goods or services—the system processing the raw materials of the organization, physical, cultural, or human. Both engineering and economics focus on the technical system. In economics, the arrangement of the core technical area determines corporate profitability. Hence the traditional array of economic variables in studies of profit: size, scale, efficiency, capital intensity.

The second and third levels of Parsons's distinctions refer to administering the organization's internal affairs and mediating between these affairs and the external environment. The managerial system, as Parsons notes, is superordinate in authority over the technical system—as in decisions about scheduling or production, for example. The institutional function, Parsons's final distinction, refers to the firm's relationship to the broader society, to "some 'organized superior' agency with which the organization articulates" (Parsons 1960, p. 63). The concern here is how firms handle broader issues of legitimation and also how they relate to outside interests— to politics and the state. Post-industrial capitalism is about the innovations related to the second and third of these areas, the internal and external systems and the connections between them.

Discussions of economic development and the history of technology make extensive use of the concept of an industrial revolution. Parsons's distinctions raise a related and interesting question central to the theory of strategic management: whether a comparable revolution has occurred in the managerial and institutional domains—in opening new routes to profits and sales by strategically managing the firm's internal affairs and external environment. The concept of a managerial revolution implies qualitative shifts in the opportunities available under capitalism. At the same time, discussions of inequality give little recognition to change and innovation in the management of information—with many social science disciplines content to restrict the analysis of inequality to alterations in production and machine technology.

2. *Resources Under Post-Industrial Capitalism: Knowledge and Information.* A second idea central to post-industrial capitalism is that managerial strategies are discernible empirically—that they can be subject to empirical test and validation and that this knowledge can be used by managers to advance corporate interests. This supposition is at the root of the enormous escalation in business-related research and in the mushrooming explosion of management programs today.

Business knowledge today is an academic concern, a field of intellectual endeavor. Knowledge is created, reviewed, systematized, and discussed in universities where full-time professionals research issues related to managing hostile environments and developing consumer loyalties, as well as to profits, sales, and costs. Knowledge of business activity draws on specialized theories, principally in applied economics, organizational behavior, and ancillary fields. These theories are typically systemic in orientation. Strategy and structure are seen as interdependent and related to environmental conditions. Organizational theory outlines options for personnel systems; psychology unravels consumer preferences and alternatives for persuasion. Corporations also draw on social psychology, political science, and sociology to collect and use information to manage public opinion, to obtain passage of relevant legislation, and to control traditional adversaries, particularly labor unions.

This knowledge increasingly is empirically based. It uses the comparative method. The studies are sophisticated methodologically, using statistical models as in portfolio models, experience curves, market structure analysis, and technological forecasting. The ideas tested are abstract and theoretically advanced, making eclectic use of the social sciences. Does innovation provide a competitive edge? What is the best point of entry into international markets? Do acquired firms perform better than those that have not been acquired? Does the multidivisional organization increase cash reserves? What currency fluctuations allow for optimal profits and optimal production schedules? These topics are translated into the business curriculum, providing a foundation for training professionals and managers.

Early on, the pursuit of business knowledge was bannered under the concept of *operations research*. Many of these ideas reflected the heritage of *scientific management* and were grounded in technical engineering. More recently, corporations use a wide variety of information reflectively and interactively to facilitate business and managerial functions (Henderson and Venkatraman 1992; Scott Morton 1991). Corporations devote enormous resources to gathering and analyzing the information common to the everyday affairs of business: scanning and evaluating information routinely on finances, sales, products, patents, competitors, markets, budgets, and consumer preferences—to survey costs and performance; using this information to support planning and competitive strategies; and making use of this information for everything from testing products and markets to controlling inventories, customers, finances, issues, and publics. Managers use much of this information in a way that goes beyond simple algorithms, employing expert systems to generate complex rules and decision criteria. Highly specialized markets are identified and analyzed. Computer networking is used to manage the organizational enterprise itself: to integrate organizations into complex unities of functions, geographical markets, and products—allowing for flexibility without sacrificing economies of scale (Child 1987; Tushman and Nadler 1986; see also the discussion of matrix systems and multinational strategies in Chapter 3).

3. *Resources Under Post-Industrial Capitalism: The Structural and Organizational Context of Business.* As knowledge about organizational processes and economic life expands, understanding increases about the complexity and alternatives for competitive strategy. This understanding focuses on strategic management. Chandler's (1977) research on the multidivisional organization typifies the themes and concerns of this research tradition. Chandler distinguished between two types of managerial functions—operational and strategic. *Operational* referred to decisions in the daily activities of business, whereas *strategic* referred to longer-term plans and designs. The implementation of this distinction, in Chandler's view, allowed large-scale corporations to attend to different and detailed fields—to different products, different regions, different markets. More attention consequently could be given to contingencies, forsaking global strategies for situational advantage, and forsaking unitary bureaucratic organization for hybrid structures with less centralization of power and greater managerial discretion.

Chandler implied that there was continued tension between two forces: (a) the scale economies derived from mass producing or distributing a single product, and (b) the attention necessary to compete in highly differentiated environments, giving attention to nuances in demand, in competition, in customers, customs, and politics. Current thought, organized around the idea of strategic management, also emphasizes this tension in underlining the contingent nature of managerial strategy and specifying propositions and policy according to the different environments or markets businesses face. This view stresses the complexity of economic life. Owing to variation in locales, cultures, products, and politics, strategies are contingent on place, time, and circumstance. These ideas also stress the importance of planning to continuously examine the fit between strategy and organizational structure (Ansoff 1965; Oster 1990). The

ideas suggest multiple strategies business may pursue simultaneously, strategies designed to meet whatever competition demands.

The implication of this supposition—of a distinctive strategy and
a distinctive structure, best fit for a particular environment—is related to a proliferation in organizational forms. Recent theorists,
alternatively, highlight the "iron cage of bureaucracy" and argue that
bureaucracies predominate today (DiMaggio and Powell 1983). But
recent developments in the capitalist firm are not about bureaucracy.
They are about an expanding variety of organizational forms and
strategic alliances that are at the same time large and small, centralized and decentralized, bureaucratic and nonbureaucratic, long-
lasting and ephemeral. In post-industrial capitalism, bureaucratic
routine diminishes. The decline reflects many of the organizational
types discussed by managerial gurus prophesizing innovations and
pleading for change (Kanter 1983; Leavitt 1986; Peters and Waterman
1982). They also reflect the increased awareness among organizational
theorists of the problems of bureaucratic structure and the many
alternatives to the monolithic bureaucracy (Hage 1988; Heydebrand
1989; March and Simon 1958).

By highlighting contingent strategies, organizations at once depart
from bureaucratic routine and at the same time require more managerial and professional input. That is, as uniform and global rules
decline in importance, more professional and managerial expertise
is needed to guide the decision making requiring discretion and
informed judgment (Blau et al. 1966). Professionals reduce bureaucratic routine. They provide flexibility and adaptability in lieu of
rules and central authority. They allow businesses to capitalize on
size and scale and at the same time attend to technical detail and to
diversity in different markets and in different areas of concern.

From this view, it is no coincidence that professionals and managers in business have escalated dramatically in recent years in a way
that has little to do with the industrial shift to a service economy
(Wright and Martin 1987). In manufacturing, for example, the proportions of professionals and managers increased from 3% and 4%
in 1940 to 12% and 14% in 1990 (U.S. Bureau of the Census 1943, pp.
233-34; U.S. Bureau of the Census 1992, pp. 160, 168). The accelerating
proportion of managers and professionals within the business community is a consequence both of the decline in family management
and the increased functional importance of these managers in a
system stressing discretion rather than across-the-board judgments.

These three developments are the kernel of recent alternatives in capitalism: an expanded domain for managerial activity, a wider base of knowledge for understanding markets and corporations, and a more flexible organization capable of translating managerial and professional discretion into competitive advantage. These developments propel the virtual explosion in managerial activity over the last 50 years. They support the increased attention to the *process* of production and sales, rather than just to the *product* as such—giving concrete meaning to Drucker's (1992) assertion that business organizations are less frequently structured around the production and distribution of commodities and more frequently around the dissemination of information and ideas.

A Note on Business Rationality

Many people have criticized allegations of formal rationality in the business enterprise. They note the difficulties in sustaining rationality across the vast domain of corporate activities and point to the frequent substitution of myth and ritual for efficiency and rationality (Meyer and Rowan 1977; Powell and DiMaggio 1991; Scott and Meyer 1991; Simon 1957). Many of these analysts characterize business knowledge as "hype" and dismiss managerial strategies as "flavor of the month managing" (Eccles et al. 1992; Luttwak 1994; Nohria and Berkley 1994). In these views, rhetoric abounds, with trends in managerial strategies reflecting simply fad and fashion. More cynical observers see schools of management as vocational centers—offering nothing more than the Willy Loman formula of a shine, smile, and handshake as the keys to business success.

Business is a social activity. In all social activity, ritual and ceremony exist. In many instances, rituals are costly because they lead corporations up roads with no profitable exit (Davis et al. 1994). At the same time, the alleged irrationality of business is not a foregone conclusion. Numerous writers harbor a different perspective, asserting that business knowledge is vital in shaping and defining the challenges of the modern corporation (Kochan and Useem 1992; Scott Morton 1991). In my view, it is folly to dismiss all business knowledge as "pop theory" useful only for staging presentations widely broadcast in "corporate briefings, workshops, and retreats" (Luttwak 1994, p. 3). These views simply ignore the extensive use of advanced techniques for analyzing everything from corporate finances to consumer preferences. Most social scientists are well aware, for example, that sophisticated sampling frames and questionnaire design—widely used in marketing research—were hardly in use prior to World War II.

In thinking about technical advances, I follow Giddens's (1990) view of knowledge as fundamental to all that is modern in contemporary society. Giddens suggests that the key to knowledge is not only in its content but in generating reflexivity, that is, in proliferating alternatives and in inducing thought and consideration as to how the world is put together and how it works. Although managers probably ignore much that is written in professional journals, and likewise may fall prey to various flavors of the month—the input of business knowledge in newspapers, mass magazines, and more specialized periodicals increases reflexivity, increases the ability to think about strategy and plans, and, more than in the past, consumes more organizational time, resources, and energy to consider alternatives for elevating sales and profits. This does not mean that the strategies chosen are necessarily the most efficient or most rational. In this sense, Simon's (1957) metaphor of "muddling" may be apt. But corporations do accomplish many of their goals. Profits and sales are enhanced and—as I will argue in succeeding chapters—key aims are accomplished in increasing economic competitiveness and social control.

From this view, the rituals of business persist alongside increased understandings and appreciations of empirically based comparisons, involving approximations to causal reasoning and generating alternatives to more traditional strategies. Although managerial strategies were certainly part of the past, today they are attended to differently—more systematically, more carefully, more rationally, less casually. The argument here is *not* that businesses are rational and efficient, that managers are knowledgeable, and that expertise abounds; it is only that these factors have increased in comparison to the past. The key developments are the resources themselves, as indicated by the growth in managerial expertise, the expanding knowledge base, and the enlarged professional character of business administration. My argument is that these developments affect the conduct of business by increasing competition, reducing production costs, and expanding inequality.

INEQUALITY AND COMPETITION IN
POST-INDUSTRIAL CAPITALISM

My argument follows Weber on rational capitalism and Schumpeter on business innovation. But the argument looks to different events. My aim is to show how advances in knowledge connect business activity to inequality by altering competition and affecting developments in the labor force, world economy, political structure, and welfare state. Specifically, I focus on three important events:

1. A managerial revolution
2. Increased competition
3. Increased inequality

I argue that these three developments are related to the fact that the managerial revolution facilitates an increase in competition, and increased competition in turn exacerbates inequality. Although there is consensus on each of these separate developments, analysts either dismiss them or ignore the causal links between them.

To illustrate how scholars slight these causal links, consider a recent *Harvard Business Review* article entitled "Whatever Happened to the Take-Charge Manager?" In this article, Nitin Nohria and James Berkley (1994) note sharp changes over the last 10 years in the rise of the management industry and the competitive decline of American businesses. They cite convincing statistics on the rise of a management industry, showing increases in business media, consulting firms, and corporate training. In competition, the trends and evidence show America's share of world sales declining from 1960 to 1990 in automobiles, banking, chemicals, computers, electronics, textiles, and iron and steel (Franko 1991). These statistics, they argue, suggest a paradox: Why did competitiveness decline if more managers are spending more time using more resources than ever before? My argument is that the causal connections and their reasoning should be reversed: Competitiveness is increasing because more managers are spending more time using more resources than ever before. Increasing competition is precisely what managers try to do—to work into markets by challenging monopoly domination.

Expanding informational resources in business create options and opportunities, offering new arenas for competition not previously considered. As resources expand, competition between corporations intensifies in at least two ways. First, the *scope* of competition increases, particularly across national boundaries. As more resources become available, business organizations become more skilled in crossing political, geographical, and cultural boundaries. Corporations gain expertise in new forms of merchandising, marketing, and advertising, allowing them to compete effectively with well-established domestic firms. Also, they begin to capitalize on national diversities, taking advantage of changing currency rates, national labor laws, and local facilities. Flexible business organizations permit more strategic advantage—particularly in coupling the heterogeneous demands of competition in multiple markets with economies of scale. Domestic monopolies become increasingly difficult to sustain.

Expanding resources also increase the *intensity* of competition. In large corporations, energy is channeled into the search for competitive advantage. Departmental staffs are dedicated to planning for increased competition along multiple fronts—by narrowing costs, by seeking new niches, by forming diverse partnerships and alliances, and by offering new services and new products. Expanding resources enlarge the arena for competition to be conducted through cost reduction in technical production but also through advertising, service, financing, and delivery. Corporations more continuously scan their environment, particularly their closest competitors, for innovations in products and cost reduction. Business management firms provide inside information on the tactics and strategies of competitors. In this way, the burgeoning growth of resources offers more parties more opportunities to affect a competitive edge. The expansion of competition is the avowed aim of the managerial revolution, and there is little reason to suspect that this aim has not materialized.

Knowledge-based resources, however, are costly. They are available primarily to large businesses or small businesses in alliance with one another. Although outside managerial services partially equalize access to resources, it is the large businesses—those with substantial budgets—that are able to afford the costs involved. As a consequence, competition intensifies among the giants of industry. Resources provide selective advantage only if they are narrowly distributed. But with knowledge-based resources in management, this is rarely the case among economic competitors.

Increased competition threatens profits and heightens corporate concern for costs. From this, only a small step is necessary to account for growth in inequality. Labor costs in the form of employment and wages are likely targets. If profits are threatened or erode, businesses act predictably: They reexamine commitments to employees, wages, and benefits. Those identified as expendable are fired, retired, demoted, deskilled, or asked to accept part-time work or lower wages as a concession to the search for competitive advantage. On the other hand, valued personnel, particularly experts in business practices, reap handsome rewards. Inequality expands.

The economy is neither the singular nor the most important influence on inequality; politics also affects inequality. More often than not, economic and political activities are connected as competitive economies stimulate political policies to bolster efficient markets. But the routes of influence from politics to inequality differ. In the economic arena, competition is primarily among those with equal access to capital. In the political arena, competition is among those with unequal access to capital—pitting businesses with entrenched financial backing against unions, workers, and others with more limited finances and unequal access to control over the workplace.

These differences are important in light of the many innovations in business procedures—in control and persuasion—with implications for influence over traditional adversaries of the corporate sector. These innovations are professionally based and require continuous input. As a consequence, the resources are expensive and available to the highest bidder, that is, to more well-endowed corporate interests. But the pursuit of expensive resources also influences the style and posture of unions and working-class politicians, involving pressures to seek out well-heeled backers with risks in alienating the very constituencies they seek to represent. The use of such resources increases business hegemony and alters the political balance between business and the disadvantaged. Again, increased inequality is a likely consequence. But the political use of knowledge-based resources, their expense, and their affinity for the privileged have hardly been noted in social science discussions of the managerial revolution.

The resources of post-industrial capitalism thus afford new opportunities for economic competition and political control. The following propositions summarize the major thrust of my argument:

- The rise in managerial resources increases economic competition.
- The rise in managerial resources increases political hegemony.
- Economic competition and political hegemony in turn increase inequality.

This, then, is the other side of the explosive growth in knowledge about competitive strategies. Apologists sidestep growing inequality with allusions to the long-range influence of economic development and the trickle-down effect. Organizational analysts laud the triumph of new and flexible organizational instruments—ignoring the costs of competition to labor. Yet these costs are real. They provide concrete meaning to the connection between inequality and post-industrial capitalism.

POST-INDUSTRIAL CAPITALISM
AND CLASSICAL SOCIAL THEORY

In concluding this chapter, I must briefly review the intellectual origins of the ideas I have discussed. These ideas are rooted in two of the most powerful perspectives for exploring social and economic development, Marxism and industrialism. Many contemporary social scientists see these perspectives as part of the "classical" heritage of sociology—worthy of note and followed by a brief eulogy and a quick burial. In a different vein, Gouldner (1970) argued that these theories may be unable to comprehend the realities of the latter part of the 20th century. Although these theories have their weaknesses, they are not trivial, nor are they irrelevant. Their burial may be premature.

Marxism and industrialism, in my view, are not incorrect but incomplete. Their weakness is in their partial and selective perspective. In this I agree with Giddens's (1990, p. 11) estimate that their deficiency lies in their monolithic character, in their singular emphasis on an "overriding dynamic of transformation." The implication of Giddens's comment is that the deficiencies of each may be overcome by synthesizing these two views—by an attempt to put Marxism and capitalism together with industrialism and knowledge (Wright and Martin 1987). The theory of post-industrial capitalism tries to do just that, to seek a *rapprochement* between these two classical views.

Each theory has been widely criticized for the singularity of its vision. Industrialist theory subordinates capitalism to the driving force and powerful effects of technological innovation and change. In industrialist theory, the increased complexity of the economy charts the master trajectory of societal development. The increased complexity reflects principally occupational specialization and industrial differentiation. Technological innovation increasingly ties artificial energy sources to mechanized production, furthering productivity and in turn diminishing economic disparities (Lenski 1966). Class structure blurs into a larger concern with status. In Bell's (1973) view of industrialism, the next stage of development, the post-industrial society, subordinates the corporation to knowledge and replaces the older capitalist concern of "economizing" with a new social ethic. In Galbraith's (1967) vision, the streamlined and monolithic corporation in the industrial state manages problems of the economy, principally in sustaining growth.

But the summary vision of the industrial and post-industrial world is characteristically utopian: without the poverty, conflict, and drive for profit integral to America today. This is a world with capitalism reduced to planning and control, devoid of the ruthless and persistent search for profits. In Bell's view, for example, white-collar workers are a new resource for handling the complexity and uncertainty of knowledge and information. Bell speculates whether access to knowledge translates into power. But this speculation misperceives economic reality and systematically denies how corporations use white-collar resources to pursue profits. If knowledge implies power, it is primarily because it contributes to desired goals, most specifically with respect to economic development and capitalist accumulation.

Marxist theory cuts to a different set of events than industrialism. In Marx's view, the search for profits is at the root of inequality. The hallmark of capitalism is to "extract the greatest possible amount of surplus value, and consequently to exploit labor power to the greatest possible extent" (Marx 1936, p. 363). But this view also commits important errors of omission. Classical and neo-Marxist theory ignore the strong suit of industrialist theory—the occupational role of white-collar workers. The resources white-collar workers provide, the technical expertise they bring to bear—these are unimportant considerations. Much past writing (Mills 1951; Przeworski 1985) concentrates on an updated version of the class struggle, particularly the political fit of white-collar labor into the categorical division between business and labor. But these writings systematically neglect resources other than labor and capital: the superstructure, the culture, the knowledge component (Elster 1983). Such neglect consequently runs the intellectual risk of dismissing the jobs white-collar workers perform, and ignoring the relevance of these jobs to the capitalist enterprise.

The shifting of resources, the changing occupational base, is critical to capitalism—but both industrialist and Marxist positions are intent on keeping separate the resources of capitalism and their institutional functions. The heritage of this theoretical segregation persists to the present day, as indicated in discussions of capitalism that consider the corporate costs of organizational innovation but virtually ignore the costs for ordinary workers. Neither industrialist nor Marxist theory integrates occupational trends into a coherent view of capitalism. Each ignores the other, and the outcome is a theory of two different worlds: one where managerial knowledge and professional expertise abound but where knowledge is unconnected to the economy; the other where white-collar workers flourish in the frozen divide of a class structure split into capitalist and proletariat camps. Each theory rests content with its singular vision—its monocausal conception—of the way society works (Walton 1987).

A synthesis of the two is overdue. To separate these two views is to beat the dead horses and traditions of sociological theory. The traditions treat social processes as distinct and mutually exclusive. A proposed synthesis of the industrialist and Marxist views would remedy the respective omissions in each perspective: the industrialist failure to consider technology and knowledge in the context of an actual agency—a firm, a corporation, an institution; the Marxist failure to consider resources as more than political resources and to see change as conditioned by more than political power. Both perspectives would do well to consider technology and occupations as social and economic resources but resources located within capitalism with alternate routes for development. Marx, of course, built technology into his view of capitalist development, but the view was confined largely to labor displacement.

More generally, I suggest that whatever the dynamics of capitalism might be, whatever its crises or contradictions, the way these problems are worked out is a function of alternatives that are contingent on available technological resources. The resources are not as much constraints or dependencies as opportunities for differently confronting and working through institutional problems. Interpreting resources in an institutional context casts doubt on the technological and managerial imperative of industrialist theory. It also extends and enriches Marxian theory beyond its dominant concern with conflict and crisis as the essence of social change. It questions whether crisis precipitates qualitative change. It minimizes the role of societal conditions, giving a greater role to the decision-making processes of corporate elites. It provides a synthesized view with greater flexibility for dealing with the sharp and recent discontinuities in inequality present in America today.

CONCLUSION

The industrializing society provided experiences that shaped classical theory. Marx, for one, built his theory of class relations on a narrow band of history, 19th century industrialization in Great Britain—a time and place rife with polarization and potential for conflict. On the other hand, the industrial theories of Kerr et al. (1964), Bell (1973), and Galbraith (1967) put great store in the prosperity of America during the 1950s, giving weight to the experiences of late industrialization.

But the present and future do not simply reflect the past. In the last decade of the 20th century in America, inequality is on the rise in a way neither industrialist nor Marxist theory foresaw or understood. Sharp rises in inequality reversed more than a half century of American experience. Because such reversals are rare, they signal important transformations in social structure.

My argument agrees with the observations of Chandler (1977) and other analysts—that technical expertise and corporate restructuring were partially responsible for the affluence accompanying the cultivation and exploitation of domestic markets after World War II. But I differ from these analysts by emphasizing that many of these trends persist—and continue to help cultivate new markets that are more competitive and resistant to oligopoly than in the past. Specifically, I suggest that the emergence of managerial and professional resources in business, over and above expertise in technical production, precipitates a new stage or transformation of capitalism. These resources contribute to a resurgence in the market economy: in intensifying the search for profits in marketing and financial arenas; in increasing competition into global markets; and in transforming the political structure so as to undermine labor and other liberal coalitions. Intercorporate competition increases; class conflict declines.

Consequently, the 20th century is likely to end quite differently than it began. In spite of fears of socialism in the early and middle parts of the century, America increasingly flirted with a welfare state and enacted programs to curb the excesses of the market, such as social security, assistance to the poor, and unemployment compensation. Today, the market economy is increasing in importance. Welfare is a necessary evil rather than a humanitarian consideration; nationalized health programs are evaluated as much in terms of economics as in the care provided. The weak commitment to equality is part of the "market renaissance," signaling basic shifts in American society.

Post-industrial capitalism precipitates discontinuous change in inequality and the free market. My theory rejects as utopian the 19th-century emphasis on evolutionary progress, particularly the implications in both industrialist and Marxist positions that a better world ultimately will prevail. In spite of wide differences in orientation and in political sympathies, both theories presume that the ills of poverty will be addressed and resolved. Industrialist theory casts industrial development, affluence, and bureaucracy as forces diminishing the polarized and class-ridden societies of the past. Marxist theory forecasts polarization and poverty—but with the humanitarian hope of socialism waiting on the wings of working-class rebellion.

Progress, Isaiah Berlin (1991) has remarked, is woven into the cultural fabric of Western societies. But the vision of progress in Marxist and industrialist theories is illusionary. No built-in mechanism steers societies toward progress. Nor is it normal in the course of events for standards of living to improve. Post-industrial capitalism predicts deterioration rather than improvement in equality and living standards. The prediction is based on the growing resources for business to manage complexity and uncertainty. In the economic sphere, these resources sustain and foster economic growth in extraordinarily competitive contexts—with profits always under threat. In the political sphere, business resources increase corporate success in challenging its traditional adversaries, unions and the working class. Both situations promote inequality. In this sense, the prospect for progress, the very hope and future of the American dream, recedes with the development of post-industrial capitalism.

PART 1

THE ECONOMY UNDER POST-INDUSTRIAL CAPITALISM

Advances in machine technology are crucial for understanding inequality under industrial capitalism. These advances caused productivity to increase and inequality to decline during the better part of the 20th century. Productivity, according to Gerhard Lenski (1966), expanded the economic surplus and made ever wider pools of wealth available to ordinary workers. As a function of gains in productivity, of union presence to access these gains, and of the monopolistic position of large corporations with extensive investments in machine technology, wages for many workers increased, and inequality diminished.

Inequality diminished against a backdrop of what is popularly referred to as the two Americas: the America of the monopoly sector, with capital-intensive technology, high productivity, extensive profits, and high wages; and the America more peripheral to industrial growth, with labor-intensive technology, lower productivity, lesser profits, more modest union presence, and substandard wages (Nelson 1981). Developmental theorists assumed that more modernized industry would spread, and prosperity would diffuse throughout substantial segments of the working class. As for the other part of the economy, the more peripheral sector—the "thousands of small and traditional proprietors" in Galbraith's (1967, pp. 9-10) phrase—uneven growth or decline was predicted. Low profits, low wages, and irrational organization were barriers to growth. This complemented the other pole in the economy: an expanding monopoly sector, protected from aggressive competition by barriers to entry. The uneven development of these two sectors promised a trajectory for sustained growth and increased equality in the decades immediately following World War II.

But this trend never came to pass. Research failed to corroborate a clear distinction between core and peripheral industries (Kalleberg et al. 1981). More important, however, were two surprising developments crucial for rising inequality: a growing number of unskilled workers in labor-intensive industries, and a growing proportion of low-wage workers in capital-intensive, high-technology industries. Both events were inconsistent with developmental theory. Both contributed to the escalating wage disparities common to economic growth over the last several decades.

The growth of inequality in these two sectors is a clue to understanding recent changes in capitalism. Neither of these changes was related to machine technology. In both cases, managers and professionals used flexible organizations to overcome constraints arising from market complexities. And in both industries, more competition evolved along with heightened pressure on wages to maintain economic advantage.

The story line of post-industrial capitalism is not a simple unfolding of a singular evolutionary process. Capitalism refers to a large number of business firms in different industries, with different profit margins and in different economic circumstances. Technology—in this instance the knowledge and strategies associated with post-industrial capitalism—is broadly a set of cultural procedures adaptable across a range of contexts. To analyze innovations in post-industrial capitalism, it is necessary to attend to these different industrial circumstances.

I selected two cases to illustrate how post-industrial capitalism works. The first is the personal service industry, particularly in fast foods and retail trade. The second is the manufacturing sector associated with global trade and multinational corporations. Both industries have been popularly discussed as sources of growing inequality. In both industries, select corporations have reaped enormous profits by opening up new markets and new sources of sales. In the next two chapters, I will argue that many of the popular discussions of these industries are incorrect, and that inequality results in each case from knowledge-based strategies and organizational innovations—rather than from more traditional causes, such as the rise and fall of nations or the simple proliferation of dead-end jobs.

Knowledge and Dead-End Jobs

The Janus Face of the Service Economy

A lead article on the global economy in *Business Week* (1992b, pp. 48-50) noted the "unprecedented surge in income inequality between the most- and least-educated halves of the U.S. workforce" (p. 50). In highlighting the role of education in escalating inequality, the article contrasted the extremes in educational training and occupational skills by emphasizing

> a glut of job candidates that helped hold down pay among the 64 million workers, across a wide spectrum of industries, who never went beyond high school. Only the college-educated did well. These 54 million Americans, blessed with high skills and fortified by the fact that new technologies boosted demand for the work they do, were insulated both from foreign competition and the struggles of the less educated. (p. 48)

The details of the role of education in income inequality are clear enough. From about 1970 to 1990, the wages for workers with a high school education declined, somewhat more precipitously for dropouts than for graduates. The wages of college graduates were stable, whereas the wages of postgraduates increased substantially (Blank 1991). The details for men and women workers differed, although not in predictable ways. For men with more than 12 years of schooling, earnings remained approximately stable, but they declined dramatically for those with less education. For women, wages actually increased dramatically for workers with 12 years or more education and either increased slightly for others or remained the same.

The focus on education, according to John Bound and George Johnson (1992), is far more important in explaining inequality than all competing explanations, including the decline of unionization, the rise and fall of industries for high-wage workers, and labor demand and supply. The explanation suggests a meritocracy, with highly educated workers receiving the spoils of an unequal system. The focus on education also suggests important policy implications, emphasizing how individuals armed with educational training can fortify themselves against the winds of harsh economic times.

Like most human capital perspectives, the findings on education and income raise as many questions as they answer. Why is income increasingly differentiated by educational training? On this, Bound and Johnson (1992) are mute. Their analysis alludes to technological change, but they fail to stipulate what this change is and why it works as it does. Other analysts do little more than offer metaphors for describing these patterns. Zukin and DiMaggio (1990, p. 30), for example, distinguish between "high-level jobs" involving information processing and "low-level service jobs" involving the "Kmarting of the labor force." *Business Week* (1992c) quoted Harvard economist Richard Freeman as suggesting that America may be following the Latin American trajectory of class polarization. Edward Luttwak's (1993) volume, *The Endangered American Dream: How to Stop the United States From Becoming a Third World Country*, draws the same parallel between the United States and Latin America, arguing that class patterns in America increasingly resemble those in Third World nations.

Parallels between developed and underdeveloped countries are engaging. But the reference to the United States as an embryonic Latin America is just a metaphor—a label with little contribution to understanding. Metaphors may misinform more than they inform, and such is the case here. For example, even poorly paid U.S. workers earn much more than the working class in Latin America. Many of the poorest paid workers in Latin America and other underdeveloped countries work in the so-called informal economy. They are employed in residual work, in odd jobs and tasks that the middle class finds demeaning. In other instances, their jobs are superfluous, as illustrated in the frequency of operators and attendants employed on automatic elevators. But the work of many U.S. employees in low-level service jobs is neither in the informal economy nor residual or superfluous. Furthermore, class patterns in the United States occur in a context of a booming consumer society with widespread affluence. This is simply not the case throughout much of Latin America.

The metaphor about Latin America is misleading in another sense. It implies an economy out of joint—a schizoid operation, extraordinarily fragmented in structure: rewarding the well-endowed in the midst of an underclass with few skills and increasingly little opportunity. The understanding is of two parts to class structure, with an elite profiting from advanced technological developments and a dispossessed left behind in the shift to a high-tech world. But is this account realistic? Is the apparent bifurcation in education and income just a reflection of an unintegrated economy with one foot in the future and the other in the past? In this chapter, I take issue with traditional interpretations of the findings on education and income. I suggest that although the class structure is polarized, such fragmentation is not part of a disjointed economy but rather of a functionally integrated economy with the top and bottom both part of the same fabric, the same overall master trend toward escalating rationalization in business.

The premise of my argument rests on the phenomenal development of the American economy over the last 40 years and the increasing growth in material consumption. The bifurcated structure of education and rewards flows, I believe, from consumption and the rational structure prompting its growth. Comparative data from the World Bank indicate that the United States has maintained a consistent profile: the highest spender for private consumption as a percentage of gross domestic product among industrialized countries. The comparisons hold for all member nations of the Organization for Economic Cooperation and Development, for high-income economies generally, and for Japan (World Bank 1993). Furthermore, the differences between the United States and these nations have increased significantly in recent years. This appetite for consumer goods—and the enormous opportunities provided for sales and profits—are the central driving forces in American capitalism today, as it was in the so-called golden years after World War II.

Intense consumption, however, is not a given. It does not just grow helter-skelter—in Topsy-like fashion. It is prompted, preened, facilitated, marketed, and advertised by large organizations. Nor does it occur in a world of small shopkeepers, corner stores, and mom-and-pop outlets. Over the 40-year period from the end of World War II to the present, corporate America revolutionized the structure of personal services and retail trade. Forty years ago, fast-food outlets were hardly apparent, and shopping centers were virtually nonexistent. Although numerous retail outlets were well-developed—Woolworth, Sears, Kresge, and Wards—few had the volume of sales and the fierce, driving competitiveness associated today with discounters of the Kmart and Wal-Mart variety.

Zukin and DiMaggio mention the "Kmarting of the labor force," but this phrase fails to capture fully what is at issue. In part, capital in retail trade and personal services became more concentrated over the last several decades. But the entire industry became more rationalized as well. In Theodore Leavitt's (1986) phrase, rationality involved the industrialization of services, the emulation of rationality in manufacturing. Activities were routinized into protocols by managers and professionals expert in bringing to services the same skills and expertise that an earlier generation brought to the factory. In this sense, the growth of business rationality discussed in the last chapter had its most noticeable effect in the very sectors where rationality has been least present in the past. Here the rationalization of business practices has been overwhelming, turning an industry of small shopkeepers into national franchises, chains, and other networks of corporate alliance. These developments capitalized on a growing affluent population, developing a demand for consumer goods that stimulated competition in industrial sectors with many shops but little growth and competition.

Consumer demand fuels economic growth. Consequently, the enormous changes in services and trade prompted and in turn facilitated the increased affluence of America in the years after World War II. But this growth did something else. Every good produced was a good to be sold—by somebody, somewhere, under some circumstance. Goods need outlets, outlets need sales personnel, and in an increasingly rationalized industry, sales assume the form of routinized tasks: offering modest pay, little opportunity for advancement, few fringe benefits, and scant prospects for long-term, full-time work. In this sense, a rationalized service sector comes with the very jobs noted by *Business Week*—a glut of positions for the poorly educated.

The ends of the educational continuum show, I believe, two prototypical individuals: sales workers in personal services and retail trade, as well as the better educated managers who direct these enterprises. Both reflect the technology responsible for prompting growth in highly underrationalized sectors, bringing the corner stand and local variety store into a more rationalized structure common to large-scale capital. In this view, a new elite provides the very skills necessary for the phenomenal growth of low-wage workers in personal services and retail trade. The two groups consequently are not different, unrelated, and disjointed parts of a fragmented or bifurcated service economy. Rather, they are pieces of the very same cloth: an affluent society fascinated with consumer goods. The metaphor of a fragmented society characteristic of the underdeveloped world is both misleading and incorrect.

A broader strategy of sociological analysis prompts my concern with linking managerial elites to dead-end jobs. The strategy involves expanding the concept of the costs of productivity and efficiency. Growth in dead-end, nonunionized jobs grew out of organizational innovations to reduce costs in producing personal services. These innovations involved patterns of franchising alliance and were consistent with the conventional interpretation of organizational movement from market to hierarchies. What used to be mom-and-pop stores increasingly became part of alliances designed to bring both rationality and economies of scale to the production of personal services (Powell 1990; Stinchcombe 1990; Williamson 1975). In this sense, franchises reduced transaction costs—the costs of doing business.

But what this argument omits is that the reduced costs involved in transactions frequently themselves have other costs—social and economic costs to ordinary workers. These latter costs involve narrowing employment opportunities, declining wages, and growing inequality. Both the market-hierarchy perspective and many alternate organizational theories address the implications of change for survival and efficiency. But they avoid the very workers directly implicated in such change.

Cui bono—who benefits? In the present chapter, I turn first to describing the new technological regimes associated with the rationalization of business. I show how managers associated with rationalization derived material advantage from this new stage in economic development. I then consider how the hierarchical structures created by this managerial stratum, a structure rich in knowledge and business expertise, provided the foundation and context for routinizing tasks, stabilizing low wages, and proliferating the so-called dead-end jobs in personal service industries.

KNOWLEDGE AND ELITES: THE NEW RESOURCES OF POST-INDUSTRIAL CAPITALISM

The expansion of business innovations under post-industrial capitalism creates a new technological regime. Technological regimes define areas of technical advances where "opportunities for innovation are significantly enriched" (Nelson and Winter 1982, p. 409). I previously suggested three characteristics of this regime under post-industrial capitalism:

1. A more systemic orientation, involving greater awareness of organizational interdependencies
2. An expanding base of knowledge for managers and professionals to use in making decisions
3. A view of organizational structure as a flexible instrument in pursuit of corporate goals

Under post-industrial capitalism, managers increasingly supplement the emphasis on *product* with awareness, knowledge, and resources devoted to organizational *process* in production, distribution, and other areas related to increasing profits. Under post-industrial capitalism, the corporation is increasingly rationalized.

The rationalization of the corporation is related to new corporate resources—specifically, to the increase in knowledge and to the increase in managers and professionals to exploit this knowledge. Rationalization, however, is not an abstract event. Nor is it anonymous. Change involves interests. Interests require champions to advance their cause. In this way, new technological regimes give rise to (and in turn are prompted by) new elites—new groups that benefit from the regime and increasingly are situated in positions of power and privilege. Training changes, new routes to mobility are opened, and the corporation's scarce resources (in wages and other compensation) increasingly are given to those defined as possessing vital expertise. To the question *cui bono?*, the answer is these new elites. The bridge forged between knowledge, income, and wealth promotes new men and women of power. This bridge also introduces new inequalities in an era of post-industrial capitalism. In this section, I briefly consider some of the processes implicated in this aspect of elite formation.

New Corporate Elites: Educational Training and Mobility

Schools of management today are important in promoting business knowledge and in training a professional and managerial elite. This role contrasts with previous eras when engineering schools and institutes of technology were important educational facilities for commerce and industry—when Veblen's engineer was the prototype of industrial capitalism. Schools of management emphasize the process of business activity rather than the design and engineering of products. More attention, consequently, is given to strategies in management, sales, politics, marketing, or advertising and to related sources of profit. Business schools symbolize new fields of opportunity for the growing ranks of management, in training, career paths, and rewards.

Chandler (1977, p. 469) dates the appearance of professional managers to the early part of the 20th century, commenting that: "appurtenances of professionalism—societies, journals, university training, and specialized consultants—hardly existed in the United States in 1900. By the 1920s they were all flourishing."

There is little reason to doubt Chandler's observations. At the same time, the definition of professionalization he uses may be limited. My best guess is that the professional training of managers did not come to pass until much later, well past the midpoint of the 20th century. In this I follow Bell's (1973, p. 374) definition of professionals as receiving "formal training, but with a broad intellectual context." Using this definition, my judgment is that prior to the 1950s, training in business lacked a broad intellectual context. Rather it followed an apprentice-journeyman model. Research primarily involved case studies, descriptive accountings of business operations with modest explanatory aims. Business education was oriented toward practice. Skills were chiefly vocational. Training emphasized role models. Business education was more descriptive than analytical. Recommended procedures were presumed to be the best advice at the moment. Educated business men and women learned the rituals, the folkways, and the language of business (Locke 1989).

In the mid-1950s, much of the vocational emphasis in business education changed. Several critiques of business education, particularly two critical reports by the Ford and Carnegie foundations, spurred business schools to radically revise their curricula (Porter and McKibbin 1988). The Ford report focused on the narrow vocational and provincial components of business education. Foundation officials called for the complete elimination of superficial courses such as business English, business mathematics, and writing business letters. They suggested eliminating from the core curriculum courses in particular industries, such as transportation or insurance. They urged greater integration of liberal arts into the business curriculum and the strengthening of core courses in economics, accounting, statistics, law, finance, marketing, and management. The foundation proposed to increase the analytical precision of managers and increase their ability to solve problems. Ford backed its intent with grants of more than $30 million to schools and individuals to facilitate radical revision of business education, training, and the curriculum. Although many still criticize the relevance of the business curricula, there is little doubt that it is less vocationally oriented than in the past. As a result of shifts in the curricula, the training of business women and men today is more professional and more analytic.

At the same time, the expansion of business schools increased opportunities for educational training. In just the short period from 1982 to 1992, schools of management increased almost 25%—from 545 to 670 (Nohria and Berkley 1994, p. 130). As management programs expanded on campus, so did their importance and prestige, rivaling the traditional bastions of professional privilege, including institutes of technology and schools of engineering, law, and medicine. Many business schools are heavily endowed, frequently assuming the names of wealthy benefactors. Although their most notable products, MBAs, frequently are scorned for lacking everything from common sense to intellect and compassion, it is doubtful that business schools (or their products) will decline in the near future (Behrman and Levin 1984; Blum 1991; Kolson 1982). Downsizing may affect the number of students seeking advanced business degrees. The curricula may be altered as corporate interests try to more finely match their needs with what training schools provide. But both business schools and MBAs are new and important sources of institutional power in American society, and this power is unlikely to diminish.

The growth in management programs corresponds to an increasing view of business as a rewarding and desirable occupation. Astin, Green, and Korn (1987) report an approximate doubling in the percentage of students following business as a "probable career occupation"—increasing from 11% in 1970 to 25% in 1987. These demands and aspirations are borne out by the soaring numbers of students actually majoring in business-related fields. In 1990, one quarter of a million bachelor's degrees were awarded in business and management. The number accounted for approximately 25% of all degrees awarded, a proportionate increase of more than 50% since 1950. Undergraduate degrees in business account for by far the highest number among the 27 fields listed by the National Center for Education (U.S. Bureau of the Census 1993, p. 184). Thus, more degrees are in business than in any other discipline—including education (11%), engineering (8%), and an aggregate listing of the social sciences (10%).

The growth in business programs and business majors reflects and affects fundamental shifts in the division of labor within the corporation. Increasingly, corporations are driven by growing numbers of managers and professionals. In 1960, for example, less than 4% of the labor force in manufacturing was professional and 6% managerial (Browning and Singelmann 1980). Some 30 years later, the percentages increased several fold—to 12% and 14% respectively (U.S. Bureau of the Census 1992, pp. 160, 168); in some industries, notably retail trade, the proportions of salaried managers are noticeably higher. These changes reflect increased corporate attention to specialties in finances, marketing, sales, advertising, public relations, and product development. Under post-industrial capitalism these activities are routine to everyday life in the corporation. Managerial functions are considered differently: They are subject to professional expertise and advice. To paraphrase Giddens (1990), managerial functions have *reflexivity*—somebody thinks about them as a professional or under the advice of professionals.

Not surprisingly, specialized training in business management is increasingly the career path, the conduit for job mobility. Training in management is also the route to executive office and thus to power in the American corporation. Today the chief executive officer (CEO) is less frequently expert in technical production—the person with hands-on experience on the factory floor. Business thus parallels the experience of all large organizations in demanding more formal training, legitimated by an educational system and with a preference skewed toward elite institutions. In 1950, approximately 4% of top executives had degrees in business administration. By 1964, this was 17%, by 1977, 20%, and by 1987, about 23% (Aaronson 1992). Because mass business education is in its infancy, these proportions unquestionably will grow in the future.

Professional jobs in management are points of entry to elite status in the corporation. Earlier in this century, engineers—experts in production technology—were the most common occupation in the higher reaches of corporate authority. But this priority, as Neil Fligstein (1990) has shown, shifts under post-industrial capitalism, reflecting changing corporate concern from technical production to sales, finances, marketing, and other aspects of internal management and external affairs. This shift initially surfaced in corporate advertising's concern with product identification and symbols. Although marketing and public relations are still significant backgrounds for corporate leadership, they recently have been replaced with an interest in finances (Fligstein 1990). Financial tracking, financial manipulation, and other schemes for raising profits and reducing costs—all exemplify the contemporary and pervasive corporate fascination with the bottom line.

New Corporate Elites: Managerial and Consulting Firms

The importance of knowledge and strategy in the new technological regime of post-industrial capitalism is further reflected in the external resources of the corporation, in specialties related to business or producer services (Greenfield 1966). Producer services are resources used by businesses to apply knowledge to commercial affairs. They broadly cover all major issues faced by corporations, including advertising, public relations, management consulting, and financial support.

Producer services, in Browning and Singelmann's (1978) view, are the fastest-growing sector in the American economy during the last century. Browning and Singelmann estimate that 4.6% of the workforce in 1940 worked in producer services; in 1990, using the same definition, that group had increased to 15.6% (U.S. Bureau of the Census 1992, p. 396). Nohria and Berkley (1994) note the ascendence of the management industry, reflecting across-the-board increases in business consultants, consulting firms, and consulting revenues. In the decade from 1982 to 1992, for example, consulting revenues increased fivefold, totaling more than $15 billion today. These increases reflect the role of producer services in infusing knowledge into production and the increased importance of knowledge in all economic activity. Stanback and his colleagues (1981) indicate that producer services account for approximately one quarter of the gross national product—important testimony to the structural importance of this industry.

The changing division of labor in industry reflects the increased scale of resources devoted to managerial strategies and issues. Eccles and Crane's (1988) case history of Union Carbide vividly attests to the magnitude of this scale and to the importance of producer services in corporate change. At the time of their study, several difficulties threatened Union Carbide's financial integrity: the company's role in the Bhopal disaster, declining valuations in its stock, and threats of a corporate takeover from international competition. In consultation with First Boston, Union Carbide attempted an intricate and complex reorganization to restructure its financial obligations; this involved making counteroffers to shareholders, lowering corporate debt, reducing interest payments, issuing new stocks, dealing with restrictive requirements posed by creditors, and using a loan to bridge the buying and selling of new issues. First Boston guided Union Carbide every step of the way, providing much technical information in addition to actual loans. To affect these ends, elite managers drew on a literal army of bank-employed specialists in research analysis, trade, portfolio management, and investment, and on sales personnel in fixed income and equity markets. Just a generation before, many of these occupations were virtually nonexistent.

As illustrated in the Union Carbide case, producer service organizations reap advantages of specialization and scale economies. They supply skills, expertise, and experience beyond those normally available through a corporation's internal staff (Ochel and Wegner 1987). At the same time, producer services provide more than technical advice. And therein lies a most vital and important function they serve. These services, by virtue of contact with diverse clientele, survey the competition, monitor markets, and scrutinize economic environments. Producer services—lawyers, bankers, accountants—link customers to communities of businesses with common problems

(Baker 1990; Montagna 1990; Suchman 1992). They inform clients of the market situation of competitors and counsel them on options for handling specific problems. They provide technical advice *and* social advice (Eccles and Crane 1988). Producer services consequently intensify competition by enlarging strategic alternatives. Their technical skills, coupled with informal advice on competition, reflect their centrality within the business community.

New Corporate Elites: Wealth, Profits,
and the Pursuit of Competitive Advantage

Professionals and managers are the elites of the new technological regime defined by post-industrial capitalism. In Hawley's (1968) view, professionals and managers are key functionaries, with the skills and training critical for promoting and implementing innovations and seizing opportunities. Stanback and his colleagues (1981) summarized this view by contrasting the emphases on critical resources in industrial and post-industrial capitalism:

> Just as physical capital has increased and production technology has improved through a complex process made possible by yearly increments of net investment, by scientific advancement, and by industrial research, so has management's capability to manage large organizations increased through a cumulative process. A host of new techniques, such as inventory control, market analysis, product testing, cash budgeting, financial control, and capital investment analysis, have been developed, disseminated quickly and widely, and become part of an increasing body of managerial "technology." The level of general education has improved continuously as has the level of professional training for business, creating human capital which embodies the new managerial "technology." Increasingly, corporations find it possible to put together skilled teams to find ways of overcoming previous managerial constraints upon the size of firms and of innovating, financing, and promoting new products. (p. 54)

Evidence indicates that these teams of managers are pivotal in escalating profits—thus implementing the key goal of the corporation. From the publication of Chandler's (1977) *The Visible Hand* to the present, the role of managerial strategy in promoting corporate success and expanding profits is the major theme of the burgeoning literature in strategic management. The theme of these discussions is straightforward: Professional judgment and managerial strategies are not only vital for profits but vital precisely in the areas Stanback suggests—in "innovating, financing, and promoting new products" rather than just in manipulating physical capital, as such. Quinn (1988), for example, has noted that profits for multinational corporations are as dependent on manipulating currencies and costs across international boundaries as they are on production and efficiency. Other studies suggest advertising and advertising expenditures can be important factors contributing to profits. The Profit Impact of Market Strategies (PIMS) project highlights marketing expenditures, research and development funding, and product-line diversity in profit determination (Buzzell and Gale 1987). Other authors more generally underscore the role of managerial structure and financial sources on profits (Grinyer et al. 1988).

The strategic management literature suggests that traditional economic determinants of profit—pricing, efficiency, costs, capital investment, market concentration, and scale—are themselves contingent on managerial strategy. To rely on traditional economic factors indiscriminately is to ignore their strategic potential in enhancing profits. For example:

- Market share, a potent predictor of profits, affects profits in mature industries but not in newly emerging industries (Prescott et al. 1986).
- Cost reductions influence profits significantly in tightly integrated, bureaucratic structures but not in more flexible organizations (White 1986).
- Substantial variation exists in the effects of market share on profits across industries and across product lines (Bass et al. 1978).
- Strategy and structure—rather than price, costs and market share—may be the overriding issues in firm profitability (Hansen and Werner-felt 1989).

If managers and professionals are perceived by stockholders as important to corporate profits, it is only a short step to suggest that they will be rewarded and will reward themselves handsomely. The mechanism for escalating salaries is straightforward: Corporations secure profits by providing incentives to key personnel. Corporations use bonuses and incentives (primarily in the form of stock options) to motivate and control these employees—but without any permanent commitment of funds. Evidence indicates that incentives are used more today than in the past (Useem 1993). For example, using a definition of incentives as the ratio of stock options to salary, Pfeffer (1987) suggests an increased use of incentives over time—from three- to sixfold depending on the interpretation involved. Pfeffer attributes this exceptional rise to a trend in aligning managerial and stockholder interests.

The pattern of escalating salaries for executives initially was given widespread exposure by the incredible compensation schemes associated with the high rollers and excesses of Wall Street during the 1980s. In their study of First Boston, Eccles and Crane (1988) document the millions of dollars in fees collected by top bank managers in the financial restructuring of Union Carbide. Although the details are omitted in their study, other indications suggest the enormous magnitude of corporate compensation. In 1988, for example, the year Eccles and Crane's work was published, Bruce Wasserstein, First Boston's chief of mergers and acquisitions, accounted for more than half the firm's total revenues from investment banking and earned more than $6 million. Although the star system of Wall Street may now be dead, killed by illegality and financial abuse, the old-line, more conservative, and staid firms, such as Merrill Lynch, Goldman Sachs, and Morgan Stanley, had record profits in the last several years. One cannot believe that executive salaries were paltry. In 1993, for example, First Boston lost most of its top executives, Wasserstein included, because it failed to maintain high salary standards.

But one need not go to Wall Street to understand high incomes and escalating inequality. High incomes reflect the premiums firms generally pay for expertise and skills. The high incomes are the salaries commanded by managers and to a lesser extent by professionals (Sassen 1990). The magnitude of these incomes is now a common theme in the popular media. *Business Week* (1990, 1992c) reports, for example, that during the last decade, blue-collar salaries were stable, but median salaries for managers escalated dramatically; not surprisingly, they also show that senior managers of large companies earned substantially more than doctors or partners at major law firms.

Additional studies indicate that high-paid professionals and managers are located in producer service industries. Top earners were concentrated in metropolises with substantial proportions of service personnel, particularly in producer services. Additional evidence indicates that these services contribute to explaining income inequality (Nelson and Lorence 1988). The same finding was replicated in an industry-by-industry analysis of 140 industries: Producer services among men (although not among women) likely contained many high-income earners and increased inequality because of these high earnings. These results further corroborate the conclusion that inequality reflects new routes to profit as well as the new skills and expertise important under post-industrial capitalism.

Inequality from high earnings reflects the very structure of post-industrial capitalism that professionals and managers helped create: the expanding market, the increased competition, the greater complexity of economic transactions. Producer services, for example, provide the expertise and organizational innovations necessary for expansion into global markets (see Chapter 3). Foreign markets contain not only the promise of expanded sales and profits but greater competition among all firms in all countries for major talent. Competition bids up the salaries and incomes of key personnel. At the same time, business resources increase the complexity of economic transactions. The stream of innovations in acquisitions and financial restructuring operations illustrates the evolution of complex business innovations and practices. The expanded size of the market and the increased complexity in transactions heighten the value of skills and talent, further contributing to high earnings.

As competition expands, corporations reexamine costs from providers of all kinds: banks, lawyers, advertising agencies. Cost pressures add further fuel to competition among service providers for new and substantial contracts (Baker 1990). As new contracts are secured, rewards are given commensurate with their worth. It is no coincidence that across all fields, earnings at the highest levels continue to escalate in nearly all instances (*New York Times* 1990). The across-the-board increase of high earners suggests that firms in every industry, including both more and less profitable ones, are likely to raise the earnings of key personnel. This development, then, is not a simple illustration of managers tapping into profitable corporate coffers.

Managerial income and wealth consequently emerge as a new source of inequality under post-industrial capitalism. In a former era, under industrial capitalism, high earnings were limited to a small and stable group of elites. But under post-industrial capitalism, the size of elites expands, as does the magnitude of differences between the new rich and the average worker. Maxwell (1989) and others have noted that inequality over the last several decades increasingly reflects earnings at the highest levels of income. Although several factors cause increasingly high incomes, one important cause is the soaring salaries and incentives of business executives.

This pattern of inequality resulting from high earnings is an anomaly to major theoretical perspectives, particularly the Marxist and industrial view. Industrialist theory anticipates that post-industrial concerns will diminish inequality as general knowledge expands and corporations turn increasingly to social interests. Orthodox Marxists see inequality increasing, but with the core stratum of wealthy individuals declining in size. In the era of post-industrial capitalism, however, managers, professionals, and employees in producer services are neither owners of capital nor a diminishing part of the labor force. High earnings directly reflect the altered resource base of post-industrial capitalism.

I must add that although there is reason to believe that high-end earnings inequality will persist, it may not persist in the same form as in the past. Managers, if effective, prompt competition. Competition creates pressures to reduce costs. And no one, even skilled managers, is immune from competitive pressure. Important here is the widespread belief throughout the business community that high levels of corporate overhead in the United States are an important determinant of slow growth in white-collar productivity. Although managers are not nearly as vulnerable as production workers (General Accounting Office 1987), recent downsizing in large corporations, including IBM, General Motors, and Kodak, eliminated substantial numbers of mid-level managers. Recent evidence indicates that among somewhat older workers, men with high education are beginning to experience declining incomes (*New York Times* 1994). This finding suggests that the initial observations cited in the introduction to this chapter—on escalating disparities in earnings among variously educated workers—may have temporal limits. The results also suggest the old image of competitive capitalism: a snake biting its own tail.

Whatever the future holds, this much should be clear: Consistent with the view of post-industrial capitalism as a new technological regime, managers grow in number and in importance—reflecting new directions for profits and sales. Managerial training has been altered. The division of labor within corporations has grown and become increasingly specialized. And corporations today have new career paths and new men of power. The effects of these many changes on inequality are widespread, not only in escalating income and wealth among managerial elites but in opening up new sources of inequality in different markets and in different areas of industrial growth. The next section will illustrate the connection between managerial strategy and inequality in personal services. I will argue that although high earners do not directly cause poverty to increase, the same trends responsible for escalating the salaries of managers and professionals are involved in increasing the proportion of low earners and dead-end jobs.

RATIONALIZING THE PERIPHERY: GROWTH, INEQUALITY, DEAD-END JOBS

The escalating salaries for managers and professionals is one part of inequality under post-industrial capitalism. The increasing proportions of poorly paid workers is another. In 1980, the poorest two fifths of American families earned 16.7% of total income. Seven years later, this declined to 15.4% (U.S. Bureau of the Census 1991). The decline primarily reflected an increase in full-time workers earning poverty-level wages, rising from 12.1% in 1979 to 18% in 1990 (*New York Times* 1992c). Poverty-level wages are at the root of a new problem in American society, the working poor. Poverty-level wages increased throughout the population—among minority members, among both sexes, and among workers of all educational backgrounds. But it was among unskilled workers that earnings dropped most precipitously during the last decade.

That services are implicated in the escalating inequality of recent years is itself not news. Various writers previously noted a connection between poverty-level wages and an expanding service economy, particularly in personal services and retail trade (Lorence and Nelson 1993; Maxwell 1989). This connection between escalating inequality and services is understandable in light of the sustained growth in many service-sector industries. Today, some 13% of the labor force works in personal service jobs—in hotels, in eating and drinking establishments, in movie theaters. After several decades of decline, jobs in this industry increased during the last 20 years (Browning and Singelmann 1980; U.S. Bureau of the Census 1991). From 1975 to 1985, more service jobs were added in the food and beverage industry, according to William Wilson (1987, p. 42), than "the total number of production jobs currently available in the combined automobile, steel, and textile industries."

Many of these positions offer little opportunity for advancement and pay no more than welfare (Jencks 1992). Earnings in personal services and retail trade are extremely unequal. And both industries contain proportionately more low-income earners than all other industries, including agriculture (Grubb and Wilson 1989; Nelson and Lorence 1988). These industries consequently contribute to the new inequality emerging under post-industrial capitalism, the incidence of the working poor.

What is new (and news) about the working poor is their connection to corporate growth—to industries in the core sector rather than in the margins of a peripheral, undermodernized economy. In this section I discuss primarily the fast-food industry. Fast-food firms and other personal services illustrate how low-end jobs proliferate under post-industrial capitalism and how rationalization breeds inequality. Personal services are frequently the favorite whipping post of many critics of American society, hostile not only to the proliferation of "hamburger flippers" but to the haphazard way these services have cluttered (and homogenized) the landscape. But few have explained how exactly this source of low-income jobs came about and how precisely these jobs emerged as a growth point in the economy.

The reasons for growth in personal services are by no means apparent. Both Marxist and industrialist perspectives, for example, predict low growth for such industries, particularly in comparison to large, monopoly-based industries with substantial resources and unbridled finances available for expansion. Underrationalized low-wage, high-cost sectors simply were not viewed by sociological theorists as growth points in the economy (Edwards 1979; Gordon et al. 1982). Furthermore, no one would argue that culinary excellence or a voracious national appetite for hamburgers or pizza played much of a role in expansion.

To understand the growth in fast-food industries and in the expansion of the working poor, more credence, I suspect, could be put in explanations emphasizing growth as a function of changes in American society—affluence, gender roles, and household composition. The decline in family functions traditionally prompts growth in secondary institutions, particularly in restaurants. More women are working today than ever before; there are more single households than in the past; and, increasingly, teenagers, who are themselves core workers in fast-food services, both have surplus income to spend and welcome McDonald's, Pizza Hut, or Burger King as places to "hang out."

But there is more to growth in personal services than meets the eye. Many economists look askance at the argument linking service growth to affluence. Although it is a common belief that personal services simply increase in affluent societies, cross-cultural research suggests that this may not be the case (Kravis 1985; Kravis et al. 1983; Ochel and Wegner 1987; Summers 1985). At the same time, I doubt that arguments alluding only to increasing demand—by virtue of growing affluence, changing demographics, or rapid shifts in household composition—can explain growth in fast-food services. Rapid industrial growth requires a particular organizational shape and form. The extraordinary growth in food services probably could not have occurred through a simple multiplication of the mom-and-pop restaurants populating the United States in the years after World War II.

In this section, I argue that the centerpiece of this extraordinary growth is not the low-skilled, poorly educated labor force—the most visible part of fast-food establishments, but rather a hybrid organization incorporating these characteristics into a firm long on professional expertise and managerial skills. Hybrids combine elements from different organizational types—large and small, bureaucratic and nonbureaucratic, professional and production based. The argument here is that hybrid organizations were able to take advantage of changes in American society and direct growth in a way that altered the eating habits of the American public and at the same time proliferated low-wage jobs. The hybrid organization folds low-wage workers into an organization rich in managerial skills. According to this view, no contradiction exists in an economy with poverty wages and high-level professionals and managers in business.

Dilemmas of Personal-Service Sector Growth

Theorists use the concepts of rationality and authority to understand problems in changing organizational structure (Blau 1963; Udy 1958). These concepts frame the issues faced in the expansion of personal services. Consider first the concept of rationality—the problem of bringing together an appropriate structure to enhance the probability of increasing sales and profits. Before and immediately after World War II, food and beverage services were primarily small, and many owners were self-employed, suggesting that entrepreneurial capitalism was the standard throughout the industry.

Early and detailed ethnographies of these small businesses indicate the irrationality widespread in personal services. They also
indicate the multiple difficulties these services faced in attaining
profitability. Based on loosely held kinship principles, the internal
organization of food and beverage establishments followed family
lines without attention to expertise. Commercial ignorance was common; few owners understood how businesses worked (Mayer and
Goldstein 1961). These ethnographies indicate that small business
owners often lacked the expertise, knowledge, and information necessary for commercial success. Irrationality seemed to be the rule
rather than the exception. Details were ludicrous, ranging from
restaurants with no food to serve, major repairs made without charges,
and working capital of no more than a few dollars. Furthermore, the
reasons for opening a business were frequently unrelated to business
experience or expertise. A British study cited the desire to be independent, "one's own boss," as the chief reason for entering business
(Bechofer et al. 1971). Mayer and Goldstein (1961) report that working for oneself was the primary reason for entering business, and
making "real" money was the most important secondary reason. The
assumption many business owners made is that businesses run
themselves. But in light of the abysmal success rate of small businesses, this assumption was rarely correct.

Managers in growing organizations usually respond to problems
of irrationality by tightening authority. This is the classic bureaucratic response. But for several reasons, this response may not be
suited to facilitating the soaring growth in fast-food services. Various
services, particularly personal services, have what might be called,
for want of a better word, "localization" problems. That is, the
product dispensed and sold is created at the moment of sale. Services
are intangible. Customers interact with suppliers to fashion services,
and, more often than not, the services are produced and consumed
simultaneously. Because much is occurring in the transaction to
produce the service, efficient organizations allow some discretion to
be exercised at the point of production, distribution, and sale.

Additional reasons suggest that highly centralized authority may
be inefficient for rationalizing management. Restaurants are situated
across local neighborhoods. Although exceptions are many, most
patrons use restaurants in conjunction with other activities such as
shopping, work, school, or attending a recreational function. Restaurants consequently are more numerous than other retail stores. They

also are less centrally located. Attempts to centralize authority must then account for multiple environments and markets. Also, restaurants sell perishable items with inventories that demand careful managerial surveillance—much more so than other retail outlets. Each of these factors suggests a less authoritarian, more decentralized structure allowing ample managerial discretion.

Centralized authority cuts two ways—one allowing for managerial discretion, the other involving problems in surveillance and control. Organizational analysts refer to surveillance and control as an "administrative efficiency problem" (Carney and Gedajlovic 1991). Owing to the large number of outlets, food and beverage establishments multiply the difficulties of managerial surveillance. These difficulties involve the procedures necessary to monitor managers effectively in thousands of small shops scattered in metropolitan neighborhoods, in suburban malls, and along freeways in and around rural communities—each with their own microenvironment of local regulations, different customer tastes, and wide diversity in sales and demand. Traditional sales data alone do not differentiate between market conditions and managerial effort. Consequently, these data are inappropriate for properly monitoring managerial initiative.

These, then, are the problems of authority and rationality faced by growth in fast-food services: increasing business rationality and at the same time providing a format for discretion and efficient control over local management. The problems are put in bold relief in considering the large number of outlets associated with any firm in fast foods: 10,800 Pizza Huts, 8,600 McDonald's restaurants, 5,700 Subway shops, and so forth, extending to the myriad fast-food logos dotting every nook and cranny of America. How can so vast an enterprise be managed?

The Franchise as a Hybrid Organizational Form

The franchise is one solution to the problems of authority and rationality in coordinating food outlets. Today, fast food and franchises are almost synonymous—although neither is of recent origin. Fast-food outlets started much earlier in the century, as indicated by White Castle Hamburgers and A & W Root Beer, for example. Franchises also appeared early in the marketing of drugs (particularly by the Liggett Corporation) and in the distribution and sale of automobiles. Many early forms of subcontracting in manufacturing also involved some variant of franchising principles.

In recent years, the number of franchises has escalated dramatically. Some are owned by individuals, others by large corporations with exclusive rights to entire regions, and still others by the parent organization. Franchised businesses today account for an increasing percentage of sales outlets, approximately one third of the total (U.S. Bureau of the Census 1990a, p. 778). About 500,000 franchised businesses operate in the United States today. This number is an increase of about 30% over the last 2 decades. But in particular sectors, the percentage increase is substantially greater; for example, restaurants experienced an increase of nearly 200%. Their imprint on the American way of life is widespread and profound.

More modern franchises are licenses to exclusively sell and produce particular products. Through licensing agreements, franchises tie small establishments into larger networks, permitting scale economies in the context of small-business establishments. Franchises revolutionized the structure of small businesses and the implications of size. In this way, they fundamentally changed the American landscape.

The franchise accomplishes important tasks in linking businesses to a large-scale organizational network. Some of these tasks involve traditional concerns of capital. Most important, franchises pivot on access to capital. For small entrepreneurs, franchises frequently advance capital to cover start-up costs of business. Because inadequate capitalization is a recurrent cause of small-business failure, access to capital is an advantage, particularly to individual entrepreneurs. Entrepreneurs also benefit from access to capital equipment, most notably machines involving innovations in food preparation. In turn, entrepreneurs pay an initial fee, usually about $15,000, to the franchise. They also guarantee high-margin revenues from royalty payments and commitments to purchase or lease products and equipment on a continuing and regular basis. For the parent organization, the benefits are many including sales, shared risk, fees for extending the franchise, and revenue royalties.

Franchises also solve some problems in administrative efficiency previously mentioned. The solution is simple: Investments of individual entrepreneurs increase the likelihood that owners as managers will work hard, explore available avenues for growth, and diligently consider cost-cutting alternatives. Furthermore, by virtue of their separate base of operations—even in outlets owned by the licensee or another large corporation—separate outlets are easily operated as profit centers. Costs for maintenance, labor, and raw materials are all accounted for outlet by outlet. This arrangement amplifies the effects of the market and also intensifies competition (Whalley 1990).

Most important, franchises are innovations in governance and authority. Because innovations in governance usually are connected to substantial growth (Henderson and Venkatraman 1992), they are important in understanding the development and commercial success of franchised outlets. In organizing authority, franchises are hybrid organizations. They are bureaucratic and nonbureaucratic, using networks, strategic alliances, and diverse centers, relatively independent and autonomous, but within an organizational umbrella. As with the multidivisional form, also a type of hybrid, authority is both centralized and decentralized, retaining broad authority in the central organization but leaving discretion in a wide variety of operational issues at the local level. They may contain different axes of social control, combining, for example, price and authority within the same structure (Bradach and Eccles 1989). Franchises, from this view, are an organizational structure typical of post-industrial capitalism—with a devolution of centralized authority in the context of an organization sufficiently large to reap the advantages of size and scale but at the same time capable of competing effectively in small markets.

Rationality and Competition: The Managerial Revolution in Fast Food

Franchises are also a means to diffuse business knowledge. The franchise tie is consequently a network to disseminate solutions to common problems in production, distribution, marketing, advertising, and community relations. In contrast to business networks in the past, largely mediated through subcontracting (Clawson 1980; Nelson 1975), modern franchises are distinctive in access to professional advice, information, and sophisticated accounting. Franchises inform and rationalize independent small businesses by providing access to capital investment, information on personnel practices, market studies on regional and seasonal variation, site location, construction and design of facilities, purchasing, quality control, advertising, promotional aids, bookkeeping instruction, managerial training, product innovation, and, of course, the product itself. The information system outlines the business's activity in terms of the inventory to keep, sales to have, discounts to effect, advertisements to use, mark-ups to make. Details are provided, down to specifying the optimum rigidity of seats, to increase customer comfort but discourage lengthy visits. Computerized technology continuously monitors sales by item, time, and day—providing important information for adjusting inventories and market strategies.

The concentration of knowledge resources sets the pace for the personal service franchises, staking out the advertising campaigns, the product testing, the cultivation of a comparative niche, and most of all the aggressive pace of growth that takes the fast-food industry beyond the borders of local neighborhoods into schools, airports, institutions, office buildings, and shopping centers, increasingly on a worldwide basis. Furthermore, businesses are standardized to the point where, within reasonable bounds, franchises can be replicated in multiple settings, whether in the suburbs, the South, small towns, metropolises, or ultimately across the face of the globe. It is this capacity for replication that likewise contributes to franchise success and to the high pace of expansion associated with the fast-food industry. Although critics decry the homogeneity of the franchise operation and the monotony of the national landscape, for many customers this is a positive feature of fast-food outlets. They provide known quantities, known qualities, and known prices, whatever the environment.

As previously noted, franchised fast-food outlets increased by more than 200% in the last 20 years. During this time, the structure of the industry changed. In 1972, 28% of the food and beverage industry was incorporated, in contrast to nearly 60% in 1987. During the same time period, the level of economic concentration more than doubled—with the top eight firms accounting for 7.3% of sales in 1972 in contrast to 16% in 1987 (U.S. Bureau of the Census 1976, pp. 1-116, 1-126; U.S. Bureau of the Census 1990b, pp. 1-126, 1-138).

Although concrete evidence for this judgment is sorely lacking, I agree with Parcel and Sickmeier's (1988, p. 43) estimate that "the growth of McDonald's and other fast-food firms . . . [has] accounted for rapid growth in what had been a small industry." From this view, the rapid growth and phenomenal success of the fast-food industry would not be possible were the industry composed simply of the mom-and-pop stores of some years ago. Aggressive growth requires capital, corporate planning, managerial knowledge, and expertise. This fabulous success of fast-food franchises is consequently important to the proliferation of poverty-level jobs in America today.

Franchises contribute not only to the pace of growth but to large-scale organizational competition as well (Ochel and Wegner 1987). In the past, the many small establishments in the food and beverage industry approximated the model of the individual entrepreneur common to the classical economic view of competition. But in fact, these small shops and local stores were rarely intensely competitive. As Richard Scott (1992, p. 202) has noted "industry groups with low concentration ratios are, by definition, composed of a great many small firms, no one of which is able to generate great competition on its neighbors."

Competition in fast foods is fueled by extensive advertising budgets. Heavy emphasis on advertising is an essential component of the manipulation of knowledge associated with post-industrial capitalism. The advertising budgets implement marketing strategies to differentiate largely similar products—in lines of pizza, soda, and hamburgers—and carve out a stable customer base. As the capital necessary for machine production posed barriers for entry in the manufacturing sector, the capital necessary for marketing erects barriers for entry in personal services. Access to large customer bases is available only to those with the financial resources necessary for implementing extensive and costly marketing strategies. In this way, the options and alternatives for competition are enlarged and restricted to oligopolistic giants of the personal service industry—further contributing to pressures for reduced labor costs and mounting inequality. Clearly, extensive advertising budgets were virtually impossible to support in smaller establishments.

Managerial Presence and Dead-End Jobs

The up-front labor force, the production worker, is the most salient and symbolically visible segment of the personal service organization—the tip of the iceberg outlined by the familiar entourage of teenage, part-time, and female help. These workers, the hamburger flippers with their low pay and meager skills, are the popular vision of what the service sector is about.

But there is more to personal services than part-time help. As a hybrid organizational structure, franchises are rich in managerial and professional expertise. The core of managerial expertise is housed outside the establishment—in regional and national offices that franchisees can use. This concentration of managerial resources sets the pace for growth and infuses the network with knowledge and business rationality. It provides a forum for common solutions to common

problems. It rationalizes growth by controlling new recruits, social-
izing them to franchise operations, and partially surveying later
operations.

The parent organizations consequently resemble the so-called "hollow corporations" popularized during the 1980s (*Business Week* 1986).
These are the franchise-type operations that license the manufacturing of top-line products with some cachet. These research, development, and marketing organizations are top-heavy in capital, market
skills, and managerial expertise. Although hollow corporations and
personal service-based franchises are both licensing arrangements
extending managerial and professional networks to production facilities, there is an essential difference between them: Parent franchise organizations in personal services do not rotate their skills
among varying production facilities. They may in some instances
own these facilities, their so-called company stores, or they may be
related to them through strong contractual agreements. Their responsibility for what occurs in the establishment—particularly the
conditions of employment—is purposeful and direct.

Within the fast-food outlets themselves, there are other layers of
organizational skill in addition to the usual array of part-time help.
Managers stand at every node in the intricate network of the hybrid
organization. The presence of managers within the establishment is
an obvious fact but frequently ignored in considering personal service jobs. Parcel and Sickmeier's (1988) study of McDonald's stores
suggests a high density in managerial presence: For every establishment (with an approximate crew of 75 workers), there are four to
five salaried managers and six to seven swing managers. These
figures exclude the managers and other professionals working for
McDonald's at corporate headquarters and within the divisions according to zone, region, and markets. The proportion of salaried
managers working in the food and beverage industry is 11.2%,
somewhat higher than the national average of 9.5% in the private
sector generally (U.S. Bureau of the Census 1984, pp. 1, 525).

The fast-food sector is thus rich in managerial presence. The task
of these managers is not merely to oversee employees, but to translate the directives of the central office and do whatever else is
necessary to meet local demands and competition: selling egg rolls
in Chinatown or lobster rolls in Maine. Store managers are rarely
temporary, part-time, teenage, or female. Their salaries are comparable to the going wage managers receive in the area. Fringe benefits,

bonuses, and seniority provisions encourage loyalty and employee stability. Internal labor markets provide career paths in corporations that may monopolize franchises in a city, state, or region (Parcel and Sickmeier 1988).

Knowledge and managerial expertise feed the growth in unskilled work and dead-end jobs characteristic of service sector jobs. The expertise is spelled out in managerial aids or technical protocols specifying how businesses are to be run. These scripts are the particulars implied by Leavitt's (1986) concept of "industrializing services." The idea here is that services tend to be underrationalized, and that well-run service firms should trade inefficiencies for neatly wrapped ways of handling customers and dispensing services. This means that workers are taught only simple technical skills, most of which are run with a machine or with the aid of a machine. As little as possible is left to the discretion of individual operators, and as much as possible is routinized and automated. The protocols describing performance and activity—instructing servers on everything from how to ask for orders to how to prompt for additional sales—are the technology of the service industry.

Task routinization and the development of protocols for sales and service are important for cutting into costs. Routinization occurs as a consequence of the very structure of the franchise system, a complex system to develop, but a simple system to operate on a daily basis. Protocols for operation at the customer level are fully developed, and the service center is compacted with information to the point where daily tasks are carried out by recently hired workers with little experience and few job-related skills. The talent is in the routinized protocol, the directives for management and production supplied in administrative systems.

Hybrid organizations thus polarize occupations within the franchised organization. In this way, franchises rearrange the principal components of monopoly and competitive industries, coupling the characteristics of marginal firms—labor intensity, low capital investment, small establishment size—with large firm size, large market share and a highly rationalized organizational structure. The franchise combines the characteristics necessary for successful competition under post-industrial capitalism: low-cost labor using information-grounded techniques melded into a professional and managerial base of a hybrid organizational firm. In brief, to see personal services as only fast-food production workers is to miss much of what these organizations are about. In this sense the concept of Kmarting America fails to reveal the strong core of knowledge and managerial expertise behind a facade of semiskilled and unskilled workers in the personal service industry. The concept fails to fully explain how the industry manages to generate extreme growth and poverty-level jobs. The concept consequently fails to confront and challenge a central tenet in classical economics: that industrial growth is accompanied by rising wages.

Moreover, the inexperience, poor pay, and part-time commitments do not appear to jeopardize organizational efficiency, at least as indicated by profits. Core manufacturing corporations linked profits to wages and to skilled and tenured jobs. Burawoy (1979), Braverman (1975), and others suggest that many industries forsake efficiency for greater control over the workforce. But personal services franchises do not trade organizational control for profitability. Profitability in large-scale service operations is similar to that in manufacturing (Quinn 1988). Parcel and Sickmeier (1988, p. 36) show, for example, that profits (as a percentage of either assets or sales) for McDonald's are well in excess of many of the other 500 largest corporations in America, including manufacturing giants such as Goodyear Tire, Pittsburgh Plate and Glass, and Caterpillar Tractor. Franchised personal services have charted a trajectory of growth and profit without skilled labor and highly paid production workers. This is an important development, for it illustrates how economic growth occurs—while at the same time poverty wage positions proliferate.

I should note in conclusion that the franchise is no easy alliance between large- and small-scale businesses. Franchises burden individual entrepreneurs with risk, although not all analysts are convinced of the wisdom and efficiency of this system (Brickley and Dark 1987; Rubin 1973, 1978). Also, the hybrid authority structure—departing from a strict bureaucratic hierarchy by piecing together various contractual alliances—contributes to lack of clarity in ownership. Conflicts over operational standards are frequent, as are the pressures to turn profitable sites over to parent organizations. Nonetheless, access to scales of economy in knowledge, goods, and other services benefits small-business owners: The overall failure rate is somewhat lower in franchised firms than for small businesses generally, although the growth of fraud has diminished overall success (Committee on Small Business 1991; U.S. Department of Commerce 1988).

Knowledge and Structure:
Observations on the Second Industrial Divide

Franchises are one solution to the problems of mass distribution and one alternative to large-scale bureaucracies. Other observers have discussed the difficulties large-scale bureaucracies face, as well as the potential options and adaptations available (Powell 1990)—all with different implications for inequality. In an important book called *The Second Industrial Divide*, two industrial analysts, Michael Piore and Charles Sabel (1984), offer an interesting view on new trends in organizational structure. Because their position on ascendant organizations and mass production differs from the position I advanced, I must briefly consider their argument.

Piore and Sabel see a crisis in the bureaucratic structure of mass production. Mass production involves rigid assembly lines, with goods uniformly, repeatedly, routinely, and mechanistically stamped out on the line. The repetitive activities unify demand for raw materials and specific labor skills. Because mass production is repetitive and demand predictable, fordist production is most often lodged in the familiar large-scale, vertically integrated manufacturing corporation.

Fordist production, however, starts to falter in the face of new economic problems. Fordism is rigid and unable to adjust to shocks in the economy, be they soaring costs in fuel or secular trends in inflation. Consequently, the accommodations of industrial capitalism, particularly the link of union demands to wage gains, begin to collapse. The shocks, in Piore and Sabel's view, threaten the entire system of mass production, diminishing possibilities for growth. Where growth can and does occur, it is in industries with greater flexibility, smaller scale operations, more skilled workers, and more innovation—tantamount "to a revival of craft forms of production" (Piore and Sabel 1984, p. 17).

The industrial context of personal services is different than large-scale manufacturing. But the questions Piore and Sabel raise are relevant nonetheless: Are the systems of mass production, mass distribution, and mass consumption I have described in danger of collapse? Is there a sense in which services have reached an impasse—a second industrial divide? Various analysts have indeed argued that the system of mass consumption is at risk. Although more concerned with retail trade than personal services as such, these analysts suggest that the demand for mass items of personal consumption begins to collapse in the face of growing affluence (McCracken 1988). Affluence stimulates a taste for the unstandardized—for the esoteric, the unique and exotic. In Piore and Sabel's terms, fordist production may limit responses to rising diversity of demand in fad and fashion. This development is critical. Were Piore and Sabel's predictions to occur in retail trade and personal services, the inequality that melds low-cost labor into a managerial-based hybrid organization might deteriorate (rather than escalate as I have argued).

Piore and Sabel forecast a future of customized (rather than standardized) production—with smaller firms and a more variable commitment to materials and staff. Smaller firms are better situated to cater to a multiplicity of different but limited markets. In one example of this view, Christopherson and Storper (1989) consider the implications of flexible organizations in the film industry. With the demise of the Hollywood formula films of cowboys, gangsters, and romance, cranked out by old-line studios on an assembly basis, a new corporation emerges: an organization headed by celebrity producers and directors with an organizational life only as long as necessary to produce a film. After that the organization vanishes. This small and ephemeral organization is at an extreme end of a continuum, diametrically opposite the large, stable, and monolithic hierarchy.

The quest for the novel and esoteric in consumption may have increased. But the implications of Piore and Sabel's argument for industrial change is probably incorrect. Small organizations may be a stable characteristic of economic life; they also may have certain advantages (Granovetter 1984). But large organizations and concentrations of capitalism are hardly likely to diminish in favor of small businesses, craftsmen, and artisans. It is not clear, for example, that small organizations are necessarily and inevitably more innovative than large organizations, or more capable of flexibility and change (Nelson and Winter 1982). Furthermore, many of the amenities of contemporary life, from cars to furnaces, could not be built easily, efficiently, or cheaply by small organizations. If innovations are to be highly profitable, they must be mass produced and mass consumed. This is the driving force in economies under all industrial regimes, including post-industrial capitalism.

As an illustration of this point, consider Christopherson and Storper's (1989) description of the ephemeral film studio. If the implication in this illustration is of a decline in large organizations, then it is incorrect on two counts. First, it ignores the large-scale entertainment organizations, such as Gulf & Western, Time-Warner, Disney, or Fox, that advance the capital, set the budget, do the marketing, plan the distribution, and orchestrate the sales. These entertainment organizations are top-heavy with professionals and managers. They do not evaporate after projects are completed. Nor are they communities of artisans. Second, Christopherson and Storper's illustration also overlooks the theater chains necessary to display the film itself. If a film is produced as a vehicle for substantial profit, it must be distributed for mass consumption. Retail theaters are not silent partners in the film industry. They set the terms that studios receive and themselves are highly competitive. And they are staffed in a manner parallel to fast-food vendors: with ticket takers, ticket sellers, candy clerks, ushers, all at minimum wage-level jobs.

Much novelty is increasingly orchestrated by organizations with extreme concentrations of capital, managerial talent, and professional knowledge. In some instances, these are centers for marketing and consumer research—hollow corporations like Christopherson and Storper's film studio. Although commonplace in the production of fashion, these organizations are big businesses. They are not studios of individual entrepreneurs, craftsmen, and artisans. Most are staffed only with managerial and professional personnel trading in the mass production of chic and fashionable consumer products. Most are dedicated to product development and research. Commenting on the Nike Corporation, *Business Week* (1986, p. 66) observed that Nike sees itself as a business involved in marketing and research rather than in manufacturing. Perfumes by Elizabeth Taylor, umbrellas by Pierre Cardin, slacks by Polo, sportswear by Esprit, Liz Claiborne, Ocean Pacific, and other innovators in fashion and design—these are the logos of product lines commonly associated with hollow corporations (*Business Week* 1986). As this list suggests, they are available and tied into large retail outlets, not to odd shops, not to craft-based boutiques.

In other instances, novelty is a product of the retailers themselves. Many large-scale retailers are the aggressive force at the center of an explosion in consumer goods. This is a new power in retail trade. They breed competition in ways parallel to fast-food chains: by tightening costs internally and issuing a continual (and sometimes daily) barrage of information on prices, sales, and the very latest in fashions. But they do one other thing as well. In the drive for competitive price points, the very largest retailers increasingly are able to squeeze lower prices from producers, with reverberations throughout the manufacturing industry. Although some of this is long-standing, the growth in corporate chains of specialty stores that dot shopping centers everywhere—a phenomenon without parallel in the past—has intensified this trend (Hollander and Omura 1989). This trend is an additional and highly significant factor in understanding the pressures on industrial profits, industrial wages, and inequality.

All of this is coordinated and driven by managers in retail trade. These staffs, skilled in marketing and product development, have a sense of what is expected to sell and are instrumental in detailing fashion specifications and parameters for costs. It is here that, under the guise of novelty, quickly changing styles and fashions are churned out with great rapidity. The Gap, for example, is rumored to change styles and stock every 4 to 6 weeks. Although some of this novelty may be aided by flexible production facilities, as illustrated by recent innovations in the garment industry for computer-based software to size patterns and cut cloth, there are few indications here of small craft-based production. Throughout, retail stores and their suppliers are big businesses. In this, the aim is to widen sales in circumscribed areas: in new markets, with new lines of variations, on products geared to specific customer interests.

Much has been written about the flexibility of hollow corporations in subcontracting production and in reducing full-time and stable employment in manufacturing (Boyer 1988; Harrison and Bluestone 1988). No less important, however, are the arrangements these organizations imply. If large-scale retail organizations are increasingly saturated with product analysts and marketing personnel, they likewise are saturated with unskilled salespersons and clerks. These workers are the "underbelly," the delivery system of the retail economy with the same characteristics everywhere: part-time work, minimum wages, inadequate benefits. Mass outlets take on the same characteristics in retail stores as they do in fast-food outlets: Highly paid professionals and managers routinize the job protocols of retail clerks and proliferate an industry of low-wage workers. Whatever the level of fordism, this much is clear about personal services and other retail trade: Behind the facade of diversity and novelty in fashion stands the capital and the organizational capacity of mass retailers.

These retailers are at the forefront of an expanding wave of consumerism in much the same way franchise organizations set an aggressive pace of growth in personal services. The breakdown of fordism is itself a dubious proposition. But even if it has in part occurred, it does not imply the fragmentation of large-scale distributors. Nor does it necessarily restrain the burgeoning growth in low-wage clerks. Piore and Sabel portray an arresting image of an egalitarian world of craftsmen and artisans. This image, however, inadequately describes the American workforce, particularly the proliferation of dead-end jobs.

CONCLUSION

During industrial capitalism, work moved off the farm and into the factory—into large-scale, core manufacturing corporations. In recent years, managerial and administrative strategies gradually supplemented the earlier emphasis on production. Innovations in management rearranged the American economy. Finances, public relations, advertising, marketing, product research—the full array of managerial services—are now part of the standard repertory in business. These services contribute to rationalizing corporate structure and business activities, while they chart new routes toward improving profits. But rationalization also escalates the demand for managerial and professional talent, providing fertile ground for a new elite and for escalating inequality in a way unobserved under industrial capitalism.

The growing emphasis on managerial strategies is the centerpiece of post-industrial capitalism. These strategies unlock areas of economic development, areas that exploit significant changes in American social structure—in family composition, in affluence, in gender roles. Through the use of highly flexible organizational structures, these strategies cultivated growth in local neighborhood food outlets, as well as in a dazzling array of personal consumer products. The franchise on which many of these organizational structures and managerial strategies is based is now the template for a wide spectrum of services, from child care to hotels to cookie shops and diet centers. The success of these enterprises, their indelible stamp on American consumption and leisure, their fierce competitiveness, far exceeding anything in the past, suggest their continued presence in American society. These points of growth also suggest, however, an escalation in delivery systems staffed by low-wage workers, conduits by which the array of products—what Rosalind Williams (1982) calls the "dream world"—is able to work its way into the homes and lives of Americans everywhere.

The presence of this delivery system and its meaning for affluence, poverty, and inequality continue to elude numerous social science theorists. Post-industrial theorists grasp the use of managerial and professional skills, but by slighting capitalism in the analysis of the service economy, they fail to specify how services are delivered and, consequently, fail to understand that the delivery system bears the brunt of cost competition. Human capital theorists see the inexperience and plight of low-wage workers, but fail to understand the link between the low-end clerk and strategic developments in management and administration. The recommendation of human capital theorists and of publicly minded politicians everywhere is to treat poverty with the traditional American medicine of education and job training for a high-tech world. But this panacea, important and well-meaning as it may be, fails to address the obvious conduit involving the distribution and consumption of the American dream.

The Widening Circle of Competition

An expanding low-wage sector is one piece of increasing inequality. A declining high-wage sector is another. The erosion of high-wage jobs is primarily within manufacturing, and it is here that escalating inequality is most dramatic. From 1970 to 1980, the turning point for growth in inequality in America, inequality in manufacturing increased by 13%, compared to 8% in services. Wage contracts in manufacturing cut deeper than usual for recessions (Freeman 1986), contributing to a competitive edge for American manufacturers but to inequality as well.

International trade is at the root of the decline in wages and jobs in manufacturing. But few observers agree on exactly why and how international trade affects the well-being of American workers. The deindustrialization of America is the most common explanation of a declining high-wage sector (Bluestone and Harrison 1982). This view argues that American capitalists are exporting high-wage manufacturing jobs to the underdeveloped world and that American workers increasingly are in competition with these sources of cheap labor. The enemy, in this view, is capitalism seeking to enhance profits. It does this by ignoring the interests of American workers and exploiting emerging labor markets in the Second and Third World—in China, Latin America, Southeast Asia, India, and Mexico. Wages in the

United States consequently seek a level congruent with the poverty-stricken workforce of underdeveloped nations.

The deindustrialization view is interesting. It has great popular support. It also is incorrect. In this chapter I will advance a view that directs attention instead to the core of the industrialized world as the source of inequality—to Canada, Western Europe, and Japan, America's allies and trading partners. My argument extends the theme of the previous chapter on post-industrial capitalism, but the content is different: Growth in business knowledge and organizational alternatives increasingly facilitates the entry of corporations into new markets of opportunity, particularly the markets of other developed nations. These markets offer substantial opportunities for sales and profit. But at the same time, they are more complex to enter than domestic markets, because they are protected by long-standing monopolies, social customs, and political barriers. With recent innovations in marketing, financial accounting, and organizational options, however, corporations increasingly are able to penetrate these protected domains. The scope of trade consequently is extended, and the level of competition intensified.

International expansion is a double-edged sword. In reaping the benefits of increased international trade, corporations surrender their monopolistic position in domestic markets and, with it, advantages vital to profits. Increased worldwide competition consequently jeopardizes profits, increases competition, and spearheads cost-cutting initiatives in declining wages and employment opportunities. Declining wages, for specific classes of workers, are part of what rising inequality in the United States and other developed nations is about. Inequality, in this view, is less a function of a society in battle with second and third world labor than of an economy increasingly bound into competition with the other nations of the developed world. And inequality is most commonly found not in the low-tech industries most frequently the source of Second and Third World labor, but in the capitally intensive industries of high-tech products—the industries targeted to the most affluent international markets.

But the argument on trade with other developed nations extends beyond a simple expansion of the market and beyond mounting economic inequality. Business knowledge provides the organizational and marketing technology to crack barriers to world trade. World trade, however, generates a new dynamic, an increasingly high level of economic interdependence with powerful pressures toward convergence and with important implications for the emergent structure of the world order. Evidence on this dynamic suggests a massive redistribution of wealth sweeping across the economies of advanced industrial nations. This evidence also suggests that intensified interdependence and pressures toward convergence undermine the probability that any one nation will dominate the global economy. From this view, the frequent scenario of America as a power of the second rank, passing the torch to the East, to Japan, is both unlikely and inconsistent with evidence on productivity and wealth. The widespread diffusion of business knowledge is such that hegemony for any nation is highly unlikely and that growing equality *among* all developed nations (although not *within* them) is what post-industrial capitalism predicts and what many of the recent and massive economic changes are all about.

POST-INDUSTRIAL CAPITALISM AND THE NEW INTERNATIONAL COMPETITION

International trade played an important role throughout American history, but it was minor compared with today. In 1870, for example, American exports totaled $450 million; 30 years later, exports grew to $1.5 billion. This expansionary growth, however, kept pace only with domestic production. For over 100 years, up through approximately 1970, exports and imports of goods accounted for about 12% of the total value of goods produced domestically. Starting in approximately 1970, however, international trade expanded dramatically, breaking with past practices, and introducing new competitive pressures into capitalism. Today, exports and imports are valued at $760 billion (U.S. Bureau of the Census 1990a, p. 804). This represents 40% of the total value of goods and services produced in the United States.

Not all analysts see the increase in world trade as significant in explaining recent growth in inequality. Some identify fluctuation in world trade as a given—an exogenous event—in understanding inequality (Sachs and Shatz 1994, pp. 78-79). In their view, inequality is a function of other more immediate causes such as technology, for example, rather than trade as such. But to dismiss the causal primacy and importance of world trade is to dismiss what may be the key precipitating event of recent shifts in the world economy.

Other arguments, however, more directly consider why international trade has increased exponentially in recent years. These arguments provide a first step for understanding how increased trade deleteriously affected American preeminence in the world order. World-system theorists, for example, direct attention to competition from the underdeveloped world by suggesting that world trade expands as core nations broaden their reach into the periphery. Other positions offer different explanations of expanded trade by referring to specific historical events, such as the surging power and nationalism in Third World countries—as reflected particularly in the emerging importance and authority of the OPEC nations; the rising challenge to American corporations among countries with revitalized infrastructures and newly developed capacities for production; and the devaluation of the dollar resulting from deficits resulting from America's lavish military budgets (Aglietta 1979; Block 1977).

Still other positions note causes relating to America's need for expanding sales to other nations as a consequence of increased research and development costs, increased efficiencies in global sourcing, and the shortened life of new products (Yip et al. 1988). At the same time, consideration must be given to declining transportation costs, including the increased efficiencies from air transport and the reduced costs of trading in services rather than goods.

These explanations illustrate the variety of issues involved in the explosion of world trade and America's diminished role in the new economic order. But not all of these explanations are satisfying, and some are clearly misleading. For example, the challenge to American corporations by other nations is part of the emerging global economy and not an explanation of it. Other reasons focus on limited arenas of interest, as in world-system theory's attention to expansion into peripheral nations, ignoring the overwhelming trade skewed toward industrialized countries. More important, nearly all of these explanations, with the exception of transportation costs, focus on need and demand. Few consider the resources for expanding global trade, the question of supply. The assumption is that international trade is a simple extension of domestic trade. But this is not the case. Historically, pressures on profits always existed, but global trade was not an outcome. Successful global trade depends on skills and resources, particularly organizational innovations and marketing expertise.

My argument relating organizational innovation and marketing expertise to escalating international trade rests on a specific premise: that international trade is complex, more so than domestic trade, and that cultivating this trade depends on developments in business knowledge and organizational structure. International markets require greater administrative resources. More managerial expertise is required to facilitate entry and growth and to provide a competitive edge in diverse markets, varying in cultural customs, political authority, and market structure. Complexities in world trade block easy and widespread access to international markets.

Several business-related resources accelerate the expansion of international trade and sales:

1. The managerial and professional skills for managing complex and disparate production and sales facilities
2. Producer services necessary for selling products in widely different markets
3. Organizational innovations allowing multinational corporations to reap economies of scale and at the same time differentiate sufficiently to sustain a competitive edge in multiple markets—markets with considerable diversity
4. Technological resources, particularly computers, to affect instant communication and monetary transactions

As these managerial resources were increasingly available in the post-World War II period, particularly in the late 1960s, corporations in the developed world urged liberalization of trading restraints, seized on lower transportation costs, and moved economic trade—dramatically, exponentially, and probably irreversibly—into a worldwide market.

Barriers to Entry and the Complexities of World Trade

The currents of affluence and economic growth characteristic of America immediately after World War II extended into other developed nations, although with a lag of approximately a decade. Evidence for the 1960s strongly suggests that all developed nations were increasingly affluent and pulling away from lesser developed countries (Peacock et al. 1988). Owing to the Marshall Plan and other international aid, most of these nations were able to rebuild their infrastructure in the aftermath of the war's devastation. Also, the same networks of retail chains and personal services were growing in these nations, along with their potential for facilitating commerce and demanding lower costs (Hughes and Wilkinson 1987, pp. 503-33). All of this appeared opportune for international trade. And all of it might have occurred sooner and more gradually were it not for a global depression and two world wars.

Trade among developed nations does not just occur. Growth in foreign trade is connected to an organizational capacity to address the complexity of international markets (Evans 1981; Hawkins and Walter 1981). International markets layer intricate financial problems on numerous, distant, and scattered production and distribution facilities—problems ranging from varying rates of inflation to changing fluctuations in currency exchange. International markets also are more complex and uncertain than national markets; they vary in demand and are under multiple political umbrellas. Considerable expertise is necessary both for producing for foreign markets and for breaking barriers to entry. The barriers are diverse, ranging from ascertaining the preferences of indigenous consumers to negotiating trade laws to considering the role of local manufacturers, who are shrewd with knowledge of domestic tradition and steeped in long-term association with the country. Investment abroad and the development of world markets require more than just furnishing capital or products. Goods do not manage, distribute, and sell themselves.

Barriers to entry assume several forms at once, economic, political, and social. Economies regulate trade in different ways. Foreign countries also mean foreign customs. Indigenous businesses know more than foreign competitors about local customs and are better positioned with respect to customer loyalties and established brands. Labor practices and labor laws differ. Most of all, foreign companies face fierce protectionism from entrenched interests and entrenched industries. In highly developed countries, competition is likely to be intense. Trade wars, treaties, and tariffs of one kind or another are perpetual sources of irritation, and they are costly barriers to circumvent in searching out local professionals adept at seeking loopholes or compromises and affecting political compromise and change.

Foreign markets pose additional problems in taste, although not in all instances. Coca-Cola is an outstanding example of an easily exportable item that, with little change, swept through most of the world with its promise of panache and modernity. McDonald's is another example of an easily exportable item. But other items are less clear. The key issue is whether competing products exist, and if so, what niche can be created. In many instances, no competing products exist, and a market must be created. This was the case, for example, with bottled water in the United States or ready-to-eat breakfast cereal in France. Corporations spend much time and capital every year field testing, advertising, and marketing products. Market analysis and advertising provide important leverage for estimating success. But money and knowledge affect probabilities. They contain no iron-clad guarantees—even with apparent winners. Euro Disney is a recent example of a multibillion-dollar flop.

In numerous instances, however, imports challenge domestic products, intensifying competition. For example, of the approximately 50 categories of goods listed in the Department of Commerce's inventory of foreign trade, the top three *imports* into the United States (excluding petroleum) are second, third, and fourth on the list of this country's leading *exports* (U.S. Bureau of the Census 1993, pp. 811-12). All are in the category of durable goods and account for more than one fifth of total international trade. Imports and exports to and from industrialized nations, in brief, are likely to involve closely related and potentially competitive products.

In brief, strategic decisions in international trade are considerable, more so than in domestic production and sales. The managerial challenge is to coordinate the international venture with a view to using to advantage the multiple markets, multiple countries, and multiple laws and customs. As James Quinn (1988) pointed out, for example, currency exchanges and fluctuations should be treated less as a problem and constraint and more as on opportunity for gain and profit:

> Comparative costs in international competition have often become more a function of exchange rates than of productivity or comparative managerial decisions. To exploit—or avoid damage from—this situation, manufacturing strategies increasingly must be designed in a flexible three-level portfolio of manufacturing sites, sourcing locations, and geographical markets. The sophisticated global logistics and planning networks that companies have created to manage the interface among these portfolios has become a new critical competitive weapon and source of system-level economies of scale for manufacturing. (p. 342)

To illustrate the use of the matrix form, consider the comments of Percy Barnevik, the chief executive officer of Asea Brown Boveri (ABB). ABB primarily manufactures equipment for transmitting power, although its product line extends to more than 50 different industrial classifications. The company has annual revenues of approximately $25 billion and employs about one quarter of a million workers. In an interview published in the *Harvard Business Review*, Barnevik explained the complexity of the matrix structure:

> We also have the glue of transparent, centralized reporting through a management information system called Abacus. Every month, Abacus collects performance data on our 4,500 profit centers and compares performance with budgets and forecasts. The data are collected in local currencies but translated into U.S. dollars to allow for analysis across borders. The system also allows you to work with the data. You can aggregate and disaggregate results by business segments, countries, and companies within countries. (Taylor 1991, p. 100)

All organizational forms—worldwide products, matrix, area— create alternatives for strategically managing where and how products are to be made, raw materials purchased, and finished goods sold. Each alternative introduces options for optimizing economies of scale, for reducing market volatility, and for avoiding bottlenecks in one area or another. Each follows the logic of post-industrial capitalism: being able to affect economies of scale in competition for business in diverse, local environments.

The choices among these organizational types are strategic. Evidence suggests that incorrect decisions to match strategy and structure reduce sales and profits. For example, a recent study by Ghoshal and Nohria (1993) classified environments along two dimensions: in terms of the strength of demand for unique local products and in terms of the advantages to be gained from integrating sales and production. These authors also arrayed firms according to their flexibility for separately meeting each of these contingencies, with several different indicators of firm-level integration. On average, firms whose structure strategically fit their economic environment performed substantially better by wide margins than firms with more questionable fit. The study measured performance with several different indicators of revenue growth and profitability. Other studies show similar evidence for different configurations of structure and strategy and environmental fit (Baden-Fuller and Stoppard 1991; Egelhoff 1988). The implications of these findings are straightforward although anything but simple to implement. Managers must understand the complexities of their company's environment to respond strategically; a complex authority structure is by itself not necessarily rational, offering little strategic advantage in various economic environments.

Ideal organizational types—area forms or worldwide product divisions, for example—only approximate the variety of existing structures in actual use. Few organizations subscribe uniformly to one or the other. Formal organizational charts unquestionably mask considerable diversity (Ghoshal and Bartlett 1990). Area forms may prevail in some aspects of the organizational chart, whereas centralization may prevail in others. Nor do these forms even address how markets are entered and what weights are given to variation in autonomy or control over local facilities (Hill and Hwang 1990). The possibility of forming joint ventures, subsidiaries, or more independent organizations as modes of entry multiplies the available options. My suspicion is that in light of the complexity of international markets, multinational enterprises are more variable than purely domestic enterprises over the full range of ownership and management alternatives: strategic alliances, cross-licensing contracts, joint market agreements, R&D consortia, minority equity networks, value added partnerships, joint ventures, and other ways to piece together the strategies necessary to enter into and succeed in foreign trade.

Whichever organizational options managers select, the multinational enterprise shifts corporate structure away from unitary bureaucracies with clear-cut authority vested in traditional departmental divisions. The ability of the international venture not merely to produce but to distribute and sell internationally (and successfully) is consequently based on an expansion in the essential resource components related to a greater managerial presence, an emergence of models of innovative organizations, and a proliferation of knowledge on strategy and structure. The wider availability of these resources provides the foundation of an organizational structure to exploit declining transportation costs and increasingly affluent markets in the developed nations of the world. The resources increase the likelihood that large businesses will be able to challenge monopoly control over localized, domestic markets, with the clear consequence of intensifying international competition.

International Producer Services

The international scope of producer services further facilitates the expansion of world markets. These services have depth in expertise and experience beyond that available from any single business. Producer services are connected to the pressures in international trade for diversity and innovation in product development, marketing, and sales. Producer services provide readily available sources of localized expertise and advice for businesses new to an area. Producer services also are vital to the complicated financial exchanges common to international commerce.

In tandem with the escalation of global trade, international producer services have grown dramatically in recent years. Thrift (1987) points to the expansion of British real estate interests in nearly every international capital in core countries, about 60 cities in all. In advertising, the top 10 firms in the United States bill close to 50% of total receipts from foreign sources; foreign offices of these firms are located in nearly all of the member states of the Organization of Economic Cooperation and Development, but their presence elsewhere is scattered (U.S. Department of Commerce 1980). In less than 30 years, between 1960 and 1987, the accounting firm of Arthur Andersen and Company increased the number its international offices from 19 to 115. Of these some are in capitals of peripheral countries, but approximately one half are located in Western Europe (Noyelle 1988). Similar trends in international growth occurred among other large accounting firms (U.S. Department of Commerce 1980).

The expansion of accounting resources and expertise is critical to the financial intricacies of international trade. Because of multiple regulations governing transfer pricing, taxes, and finances, accountants are necessary in corporate decisions to invest in foreign countries. Accounting firms provide corporations technical advice and draw on extensive backgrounds with numerous clients—experience few corporations can match. Tax considerations are paramount in investment, as this interview with the director of international services of a Big Nine accounting firm suggests (Montagna 1990):

> When the client wants to invest in a foreign country operation, he needs advice on tax structures, restrictions on capital investment, and the like. He comes to the public accountant and not the investment banker. Taxes play a very important part in this role. There is a lot of work

relating to new tax treaties. Just yesterday I had a West German client . . . who needed advice on how to structure sales to get the best tax advantages so as to not hinder his company's overall operations in other countries. (pp. 230-31)

Producer services perform the same functions internationally as they do domestically: providing out-of-house advice and technical expertise, as well as increasing insight into the problems of the competition. These services are points of entry into foreign markets. Cohen (1981, p. 295) lists the following tasks producer services perform:

1 To control diverse and dispersed systems of production
2. To control financial information
3. To develop global conceptions of competition
4. To organize an international labor force
5. To streamline information
6. To increase and coordinate planning systems
7. To access sources of capital

Cohen then notes that

multinationals have demanded more support from what I have called the advanced corporate services (primarily banks, investment banks, law firms, and accounting firms). These services now help companies to develop their overseas operations, to acquire dynamic companies, to restructure their industries, and to adapt to political and economic change. Thus, these service firms enable corporations to position themselves to obtain profits in a disorderly world. (p. 290)

To this I must add two things. First, vital to the success of overseas ventures is the array of marketing, advertising, consumer research, and public relations facilities to carve out the niche necessary for entry into new markets. Second, all of these functions are in turn contingent on advances in telecommunications, which provide instantaneous access to information on a global scale.

Summary: Competition and the Emergent International Order

In brief, today's multinational corporations are more complex than in the past and are more able to manage international trade strategically.

Multinationals transform markets from serial strings of domestic markets to global markets requiring intricate and interdependent decisions. Without the ability to handle complex information to guide equally complex decisions, the level of international trade today simply could not exist. Advances in management, new organizational forms, a rapidly increasing sector of international producer services, and innovations in telecommunications are at the root of an expanding volume of foreign trade and permit wide entry into the complex political and economic environments of advanced industrial nations.

The development of multinational corporate structures differentiates today's world of international trade from the more insular economies present only 30 to 40 years ago. What does this escalation of international trade imply for rising inequality? The answer parallels the previous discussion of resources and competition in the service economy. First and foremost, resources intensify competition. Numerous nations today increasingly compete in the sales and production of a wide variety of goods. Franko (1991) reports that American corporations have lost at least 10% of world market share in 14 of 15 major industries.

Also, as competition increases in new markets, domestic firms lose the protected environment enjoyed under industrial capitalism (Ross and Trachte 1990). Competition consequently places profits in jeopardy. As this occurs, corporations move predictably to cut costs, with wages and jobs a chief target. But, I must add, international competition does not necessarily diminish profits. Taylor and Fosler (1994) show that corporations trading in international markets are more profitable than corporations with products only for domestic consumers. Consequently, the rise in international trade is another example, along with the fast-food industry, of the connection between competition, economic development, and growth in inequality.

The next section considers some of the specifics of inequality by examining how and where inequality surfaces in international trade. In examining this issue, I turn to two topics that have become part of much current speculation on international competition and the transformation of the American economy: the competition of cheap labor in undermining the wages of American workers and the passage of the mantle of economic power from the United States to the East, to Japan. From the perspective of post-industrial capitalism, both of these ideas must be modified and corrected. The data show how the central issue of competition is with economically advanced nations, not between them and the periphery, and that the end product of the competition among economically advanced nations is a massive redistribution of international wealth rather than growth in a new hegemonic regime.

THE UNITED STATES AND THE DEVELOPING WORLD: COMPETITION IN INTERNATIONAL MARKETS

International trade over the last 25 years increased among industrialized nations, and not just between industrial and nonindustrial nations as some have implied. Several factors contribute to understanding the concentration of trade within the industrialized world. The continued development of capital-intensive and high-tech industries—industries requiring substantial investments in product development—requires extensive sales for profitability and for amortizing initial costs and investments. Industrialized countries offer lucrative opportunities for sales and profits in these products, in part because of their substantial national wealth and in part because high-tech products are in greater demand in developed countries. Growth in international trade consequently pits powerful corporations with substantial resources against one another, vying for dominance and advantage in lucrative markets. The full inventory of new managerial resources intensifies competition, contributing significantly to pressures on profits and wages.

The focus on trade and competition in the developed world differentiates this view from other theoretical views—most notably the theory associated with deindustrialization. Many scholars and lay persons alike widely subscribe to deindustrialization theory, and the position receives significant coverage in the media. Deindustrialization considers inequality to be a consequence of competition with cheap labor from underdeveloped nations. Yet the deindustrialization view is incorrect in many respects. It ignores the rivalries among highly developed nations, and it misidentifies the workers and industries at risk from the escalation in international trade. Before comparing the predictions of deindustrialization and post-industrial capitalism, a brief summary of the deindustrialization position is necessary.

The Deindustrialization Thesis

Deindustrialization theory interprets inequality as a consequence of a decline in domestic manufacturing. The theory lays the cause of this decline at the feet of American corporations. In their attempt to lower costs and increase profits, corporations export high-wage manufacturing jobs into the cheap labor pools of the Second and Third World. American workers consequently compete with workers in economically less advanced countries, thus driving wages down toward levels prevalent in the underdeveloped world. Although deindustrialization and world-system theory share some common views on the exploitation of foreign labor, deindustrialization theorists are more likely to stress the competitive challenge of labor abroad. Much attention is given to multinational corporations, but little attention goes to the expertise necessary to administer production and distribution.

The deindustrialization view attributes declining opportunities for employment and high-wage jobs to a diminishing industrial base. The concern of deindustrialization theory is clearly on production involving highly labor-intensive activities. Writing about the new international division of labor, Fröbel et al.'s (1980) pioneering analysis of West German industry illustrates this concern by indicating how growth in textiles in economically peripheral countries displaced core workers:

> The proven foreign employment of the Federal German textile and garment industry has more than doubled in the period 1966-75, while over the same period the domestic employment in this industry has fallen by around a quarter. By the beginning of 1977 there were clearly more than ten people employed abroad by the Federal German textile and garment industry for every hundred employed in Germany itself. (p. 116)

Bluestone and Harrison's (1982) *Deindustrialization of America* portrays capital as a mobile resource following a path of most profit, least cost. What of the workers left behind? The implication of the deindustrialization view is that as manufacturing moves abroad, earnings drop, high-wage employment declines, and dead-end jobs in personal and retail services fill the vacuum. Consistent with this view, U.S. manufacturing employment has decreased from about 26% of the labor force in 1970 to 17% in the early 1990s (U.S. Bureau of the Census 1993, p. 409). This decline is substantial and significant. The decline also is unprecedented in American history, although it is surprisingly less than in most other developed nations (Dean et al. 1986). Nonetheless, the deindustrialization view misinterprets much of what recent changes in industrial development are about.

American Manufacturing: Change or Decline?

Bluestone and Harrison inadequately distinguish types of industrial growth and decline and consequently fail to address the sectors involved in industrial change. Industrial sectors are important for understanding both the overall decline in manufacturing and the kinds of manufacturing activity exported abroad. In considering first the issue of overall decline, it simply is not clear that manufacturing activity has declined in the United States. Although manufacturing *employment* has decreased, other indicators suggest manufacturing itself to be quite robust. For example, in spite of the hue and cry over America as a service economy, manufacturing dollars in absolute terms have remained constant, and production levels have increased in all major manufacturing sectors (Kutscher and Personick 1986). The value added in manufacturing, for example, was $350 billion in 1972 and $1.1 trillion in 1987. In constant dollars, manufacturing was 21% of gross national product in 1970 in contrast to 21.8% in 1987 (U.S. Bureau of the Census 1990a, pp. 732-34). The crumbling manufacturing base really never came to pass:

> Factories making everything from chemicals to computers now account for a robust 23.3 percent of the nation's gross national product, or the total cost of goods and services sold. The figure is up from 20 percent in 1982, the post-World War II low, and matches the level of output achieved in the 1960s when American factories hummed at a feverish clip. (*New York Times* 1991, p. A1)[1]

The new data put U.S. manufacturers on a par with other countries, such as Japan and Western Europe. Although slumps in production have occurred, they have frequently coincided with economic recessions, as was the case in the early 1980s, and, consequently, they were cyclical rather than permanent.

Manufacturing employment has declined. But the shifting sectors of productive activity toward capital-intensive and high-technology products are the cause of much of this decline. In recent years, manufacturing employment and output moved out of traditional industrial sectors. Traditional industries are labor intensive, sometimes accompanied by standardized technology, sometimes not. Examples are rubber, leather products (particularly shoes), plumbing fixtures, railroad equipment, and steel. In other instances, jobs in America have declined, although domestic output has remained high, as in containers, cans, bakery products, apparel, household appliances, and telephones.

Manufacturing growth in peripheral nations is largely in labor-intensive industries such as textiles and shoes. These products are the strongest exports of developing countries. But very rapid growth also occurred in other labor-intensive areas requiring standardized technology, such as steel, machinery, and transportation equipment. In many of these industries, as in assembling telephone components or automobile transmissions, labor input is considerable (United Nations Center on Transnational Corporations 1983).

In contrast, American manufacturing industries increased output and employment in industries with extensive capital investment and expert technological development, including medical equipment, scientific instruments, and electronic components (Crandall 1986). These industries require considerable expenditures in research and development, involve significant proportions of scientific and technical personnel, and result in sophisticated products (Kutscher and Personick 1986). The life cycle of product development in high-tech commodities is short and subject to extensive innovation. The short product life increases reliance on scientific activity and personnel and decreases easy access to standardized production in underdeveloped countries. The growth in high-technology industries stems from the same macrolevel factors stimulating growth in managerial strategies and organizational innovations: higher education, greater occupational specialization, and an escalation in knowledge and research.

Growth in capital-intensive, high-technology products sends labor-intensive manufacturing to less developed countries. But American manufacturing in underdeveloped countries is not of recent origin. Trade data indicate that American manufacturing interests are not clearly and increasingly invested in underdeveloped countries to foil domestic labor. In 1970, for example, 25.4% of investment abroad was in underdeveloped countries; this declined to 24.6% in 1980 and to

23.3 % in 1988 (U.S. Bureau of the Census 1980, p. 864; 1991, p. 797). These observations concur with research indicating that American manufacturers tend to set up operations in high-wage countries (Taylor and Fosler 1994). Also, goods from underdeveloped countries are not flooding American markets. In spite of much annual variation, the percentage of imports from developing countries was the same in 1965 as in 1988—about one third of the total (U.S. Bureau of the Census 1980, p. 874; 1990a, p. 806). And it is also the case that exports to developing countries exceed imports. In brief, manufacturing has changed, but this change does not sharply depart from the past. Nor has the overall manufacturing base eroded.

Inequality and the Myth of Deindustrialization

Deindustrialization theorists ignore important facets of international trade, particularly the marketing strategies and growth of international trade among the nations of the developed world. They primarily look at labor-intensive production. The theory is caught up in the fears surrounding America as a declining power. The theory smacks of the images of American labor reduced to levels of the Second and Third World—of a new Latin America amid riches and widespread abundance.

But the facts are otherwise. Imports from underdeveloped countries do not account for escalating inequality, even though these imports have altered patterns of employment. And even in regard to employment, the facts do not consistently support the deindustrialization view. For example, manufacturing industries in apparel, steel, machinery, chemicals, and transportation have suffered substantial losses in employment. In some of these industries, productivity is increasing, suggesting that sophisticated production and technology may diminish employment. In textiles, for example, the illustrative industry used by Fröbel et al. (1980), output advanced significantly from 1969 to 1984 (Kutscher and Personick 1986). But in other industries, productivity is in fact declining; conceivably some wage and union concessions have occurred as well (Becker 1988; Freeman 1986). In spite of the attention in the media, it is not clear how serious these job dislocations may be. Wilson (1987) claims that the impact of industrial shifts to less developed countries has decimated employment options for Black Americans with few skills and little education. Other studies, however, indicate more minimal effects of deindustrialization, suggesting that workers do not lose positions in manufacturing and migrate into dead-end jobs of the service economy (Urquhart 1984)—with the inference that much job attrition may be handled simply through retirement.

Deindustrialization theorists suggest that industrialization in the semiperiphery increases wage inequality in manufacturing industries (Bluestone and Harrison 1982; Harrison and Bluestone 1988; see also Wood 1994). But existing evidence on this count is not convincing, and others are less supportive of this conclusion. Lawrence and Slaughter (1993), for example, argue that deindustrialization has little influence on inequality. Revenga (1992) claims that industrial shifts are more likely to be accompanied by realigning demand for employment than by a downward shift in wages. Still others deride the current obsession with foreign competition as the cause of decline in manufacturing employment (Krugman and Lawrence 1994, p. 47). And even among authors who claim that deindustrialization may increase inequality, there is some consensus that the observed effects cannot "account for the bulk of the widening income inequality" (Sachs and Shatz 1994, p. 34).

None of the authors cited specify the manufacturing industries where inequality in fact has increased. Detailed industry-by-industry analysis indicates, however, that increases in inequality are not in industries traditionally the province of peripheral nations. From 1960 to 1980, the rise in inequality was least steep in nondurable goods and among miscellaneous durable goods (Grubb and Wilson 1989). Textiles, leather products, and apparel fall into these categories; typically, these industries gain most of their products from imports rather than domestic production (Bednarzik 1993). On the other hand, wage disparities are increasingly in high-tech, capital-intensive industries, including petrochemicals, machinery, motor vehicles and equipment, aircraft, and optical and other research and measurement instruments (Grubb and Wilson 1989). These industries are also the most important exports in American trade and dominate the exchange with core nations (Bednarzik 1993; Riche et al. 1983). Trade and investment among the developed nations is extensively in capital-intensive, high-technology industries, because only these nations have the scientific personnel to design and produce these products, as well as the base to afford them—a base both in ordinary consumers and in businesses and governments interested in updated technology.

Heightened international trade in these products escalates competition and exacts a price on domestic firms. Cost barriers to entry protected monopoly corporations in domestic markets in years past. Today, domestic markets are more difficult to protect. International competition decreases monopoly rule. Monopoly status is a chief cause of profits; as a consequence, global competition threatens profits. Managerial strategies thus open a Pandora's box of challenges and opportunities: opportunities to escalate sales and challenges to compete domestically and internationally.

Inequality in high-tech, high-export industries increased significantly more than in other industries between 1960 and 1980. During this period, the percentage of low-income earners in these industries substantially increased as well. By contrast, the percentage of low-income earners was virtually identical from 1960 to 1980 in the industrial classification of leather, textiles, and apparel, the industries with dominant shares in American imports from less developed nations (Bednarzik 1993; Grubb and Wilson 1989).

Why does inequality escalate in industries with extensive investment in capital-intensive, high-technology production? The root cause is the astronomical expansion of global trade into core, First World nations—as facilitated by the organizational strategies and expertise of multinational corporations. In some of these instances, I should add, gains in productivity spur competition, as illustrated by the entry of Japanese manufacturers into the American automobile market. But increased trade is the medium; increased trade facilitates the ability to capitalize on technology gains and other advantages in productivity.

Competition places profits at risk, and these threats drive down wages. Competition is reflected in the convergent levels of wages within the industrialized world. In 1975, hourly compensation in manufacturing in the member countries of the Organization of Economic Cooperation and Development was 75% of the level in the United States. In 1988, the average level was at parity (U.S. Bureau of the Census 1990a, p. 849). Competitive pressure on wages should occur precisely in those industries where the manufacturing labor force is increasingly concentrated: in design-sophisticated, high-tech industries. In these industries less skilled workers are the traditional victims of competition and productivity gains. These industries also should contain escalating inequality, an estimate consistent with Grubb and Wilson's (1989) research. In this sense, the growth of

inequality in manufacturing is a further consequence of the innovations in managerial and producer functions that facilitated the spread
of competition to the international markets of the developed world.

In brief, change occurs differently than deindustrialization theory
suggests. Manufacturing has not declined. Instead, manufacturers
have increased investment in technologically sophisticated products
with great sales potential in other core nations. Because of substantial
national wealth, these markets foster extensive trade and intense
international competition. Intense competition spurs businesses to
lower prices; labor costs are scrutinized, wages decline, and inequality escalates in high-technology sectors. Inequality increases because
of competition in the precise markets where producer services and
organizational innovations spearhead the exponential expansion of
international trade: in the economically advanced nations of the
world. Thus a link is forged between inequality and post-industrial
capitalism.

THE NEW WORLD ORDER AND
THE RISE AND FALL OF NATIONS

A key problem in understanding America's destiny and the future
of the world's economy involves the outcome of competition among
economically advanced nations. In the United States today many
people believe they have an answer to this problem. They believe
that ties to the global order foreshadow America's fall and decline.
The era of American dominance, in this popular view, is gone.
Advocates of this view ascribe the alleged decline to typically American problems, from stagnant productivity to Wall Street's financial
escapades, rather than to the international economic order and competitor nations. At a moment's notice, social scientists trot out a
familiar list of solutions for America's ailing economic order: increase savings, increase training, invest more in the public infrastructure (and less in welfare), spend more on research and development,
and encourage long-range planning for American industry. They
allude to the fact that in times past, nearly one half of all goods
manufactured worldwide were produced in the United States. Today, the number has dwindled to less than one quarter of world
production. The implication is that the United States will follow the
path of other fallen countries, particularly Great Britain. Like Britain,

this nation increasingly will be populated by *rentiers* involved in finances rather than production. And like Britain, military might will be used to cling tenaciously to an era of past glory—the era of pax Americana.

The visions of dwindling American power are also pivotal in more academic perspectives, such as world-system theory (Hopkins 1982; Wallerstein 1979, 1984, 1986). World-system theorists, for example, explain America's problems with reference to historical cycles covering more than 300 years of capitalist development. In these 300 years, three nations dominated international affairs: Holland in the 15th and 16th century, Great Britain in the 19th century, and the United States in the 20th century. But domination is not forever. According to world-system theorists, hegemony sows the seeds of its own decline. Technology diffuses to other nations. Also, hegemonic nations act like monopoly firms in passing along worker demands for higher wages. But at some point these costs grow out of line. Hegemonic nations lose their edge, as lower labor costs and lower prices spread to competitor nations. The hegemonic nation declines and a new cycle begins.

In the several decades after World War II, the United States was widely considered the hegemonic power. The period preceding the war was a period of ascendence whereas more recent years, from perhaps the 1970s on, formed a period of decline. Decline refers to faltering leadership and dwindling economic development. The inability to dominate world trade is one telltale sign, but there are others as well. Productivity is declining relative to other industrialized nations. Soaring trade deficits reflect the discrepancy between the immense appetites nurtured in the era of hegemony and the reality of a nation unable to compete internationally. As a consequence, the United States increasingly is constrained to reduce labor costs to sharpen its competitive edge. Inequality, particularly among workers in manufacturing industries, is the result.

There is a different and better way to interpret the problems and plight of America today. My argument is that there is something new under the sun, a new world order, that this order is a key cause of American economic difficulties, and, furthermore, that all of this is better explained by recent developments in post-industrial capitalism than by the experiences of the Netherlands in the 15th and 16th century or Great Britain in the 19th century. Hegemonic arguments ignore the role of managerial strategies in bringing new levels of economic interdependence—with convergent effects diminishing the potential for clearly defined roles for the vanquished and the victorious. I will argue that recent international developments are qualitatively different than all that has occurred in the past, and the alleged decline in American society cannot by any stretch of the imagination be thought to replicate cycles of the rise and fall of nations.

America's Golden Past: The Myth of Hegemony

In the many discussions of America's golden past, this country was considered not only a rich and prestigious industrial power, but the dominant nation in recent world history. I previously considered some of the difficulties in discussing a golden age of America's past. The view fails on several grounds to account accurately for what dominance means—what international involvement was in the past, what it is in the present, and what it will be in the future. The view charts the rise and fall of nations in an unchanging world, with *domination* meaning the same thing today as in the past. But from the perspective of post-industrial capitalism, the meaning and substance of domination has changed. Technological advances have altered the world past from present. These advances facilitated growth in international trade and growth in a new level of economic interdependence. And it is this interdependence—not hegemony, not the rise and fall of nations—that prompts convergence in world wealth, convergence that has mistakenly been interpreted in terms of America's decline.

First, the erroneous view of the American past and its involvement in the world order. As an example, consider what allegations of world dominance meant for American society in the late 19th and early 20th century. At that time, America was already a world-class imperialist power with domination, military invasions, and political control across much of the globe—in Puerto Rico, Nicaragua, Cuba, Panama, Haiti, Mexico, the Dominican Republic, Alaska, Hawaii, Guam, the Philippines, Midway, and numerous other islands scattered across the Pacific. Yet in spite of this tainted record, political involvement does not clearly surface as a core explanation of early economic development. In fact, foreign trade accounts for very little in the growth period from the late 19th to the mid-20th century in America. General imports were about 8% of gross national product in 1870, 4% in 1900, 3.4% in 1930, and 3% in 1960 (U.S. Bureau of the Census, 1977: U201-6). Exports likewise were stable throughout: 6.2% in 1870, 6.5% in 1900, 4.2% in 1930, and 4.1% in 1960. These statistics suggest a nation turned inward, isolated from trade and from the world economy.

Economic histories of the United States support this interpretation of economic isolation. Commenting on the growth period of the early to mid-20th century, Heilbroner and Singer (1984, p. 344) remark that during this period, the "United States economy was a 'closed system,' reliant to a modest extent on exports, more or less indifferent to the volume of imports." Bryant and Dethloff (1983) characterize this period in terms of economic integration resulting from the growing use of automobiles, from government-built roads, and from an intercity trucking system that began to surpass freight trains as cheap transit for small- and medium-sized goods. Chandler (1977) argues that the late 19th century provided the infrastructure, chiefly in transportation and communication, for later developments in multidivisional corporations. But throughout this period, growth was primarily in domestic rather than in international trade.

In brief, international trade in the period prior to World War II and up through the 1950s was minimal, at least by current standards. If America was the hegemonic power at that time, dominating the world and dominating world trade, this power rested on an extremely slim volume of international exchange. The golden age of American hegemony, to the extent it ever existed, took place at a time and place different than the world today. For over 100 years, up through approximately 1970, exports and imports of goods accounted for a minor proportion of the total value of the goods produced in the United States, in sharp contrast to the present (U.S. Bureau of the Census 1990a, p. 804). Similar trends are indicated with respect to investments, with foreign investments increasing from the 1960s to the 1980s more than 20 times, at the same time that the gross national product increased, by comparison, between 8 and 9 times (U.S. Bureau of the Census 1990a, p. 793). These statistics imply that the era of America's so-called golden past coincided with comparative economic insularity, and the period of America's alleged decline coincided with greater economic interdependence in world trade. The evidence thus suggests that observers may actually be seeing the consequences of economic interdependence in a world order rather than the rise and fall of nations.

Convergence or Decline: The Future of Hegemony

The rise and fall of nations is an arresting idea, as reflected in persistent fascination with the works of Toynbee (1935), Spengler (1926), and Sorokin (1937). But conceptions of rise and fall, and the related concept of hegemony, may be outmoded for analyzing today's global economy. In the past, hegemony resulted from domination and mastery of key innovations in technology. But the technology I have discussed here—broadly based on knowledge and widely available in academic journals and texts—is more easily diffused than technology involving engineering and production. In a world of student exchange, scientific publication, and scholarly conferences, innovations in organizational structure and business knowledge are difficult to monopolize. Managerial strategies are widely available by subscribing to producer services of one sort or another. They can be implemented by many organizations with access to the capital to hire the expertise necessary for molding competitive strategy. These strategies are within easy reach of major corporations in all of the wealthy nations of the world.

Difficulties also confront any corporations in these nations that attempt to monopolize productive technology. Most technology does not devolve on a single innovation or invention. Although technical secrets can be guarded, they are themselves subject to business rationality. Elaborate databases are used increasingly to minimize secrecy by tracking the patents of domestic and foreign competitors for clues to rival technological development. At the same time, the life cycle of innovations is shortening.

Hegemony also may be too categorical a concept to describe the contemporary world economy. Can any single country dominate all arenas of world competition? Although Japan is widely considered the new hegemonic power, the facts suggest otherwise. Productivity is unevenly distributed—higher in some cases in the United States, higher in other cases in Japan, Germany, or other countries. Nor is it clear that dominance today is aptly reflected in national terms. Increasingly multinational firms blur national allegiances. At the same time, regional alliances such as the North American Free Trade Agreement (NAFTA) and the European Economic Community (EEC) suggest prospects in the devolution of national boundaries. These trends eclipse hegemony for any nation, the United States and Japan included (Baumol et al. 1989).

In fact, a case can be made to the contrary, in opposition to hegemony: The evidence on supranational relations increasingly suggests an emergent global order centered in core nations. For example, provisions in the EEC or NAFTA regulate production, ownership, and currency transactions across national borders. The breakdown of national peculiarities in financial regulations and increased pressures within nations to conform to standards of others are added indicators of the internationalization in markets. Firms and banks in core nations increasingly resemble one another in magnitude of assets (Fenneman and van der Pijl 1987). Corporations also increasingly relate to one another across national boundaries, as suggested by the increasing proportion of international interlocks among boards of directors at the same time that domestic interlocks are constant (Fenneman and van der Pijl 1987).

Trends in financial markets further aid in understanding what world trade and interdependence are about and strongly suggest an emergent international order. For example, Eurocurrencies, particularly Eurodollars, signify the internationalization of capital and may be transitional in the development of an international currency. As Robert Cohen (1981) has noted,

> [the] financial network facilitates the management and development of ever more far flung centers of operations by multinational corporations. It also provides them with greater flexibility in their adaptation to any new political and economic changes which occur in different parts of the world. (p. 290)

Financial markets did not exist 20 or 30 years ago as they do today (Hymer 1971). In this the last decade of the 20th century, financial markets account for the lion's share of all economic transactions. For example, exchange in world financial trade and options contracts developed only recently. In 1975, $0.2 billion were traded in futures compared to $439 billion dollars in 1986. With respect to options, the figures were less than $1 billion in 1975 compared to $294 billion in 1986 (Levich and Walter 1990). Over a 10-year period, from 1980 to 1990, investments in international stock markets increased from $19 billion to $309 billion (Smith 1990). Trade in foreign currencies in New York in the 1980s was 10 times the level of the 1970s (Levich and Walter 1990). These transactions track enormous movements of wealth. Levich and Walter (1990) estimate that currency trading in

1990 was nearly $60 trillion, an amount exceeding world trade and world gross national product.

Given the immense sums involved in international investment and trade, these exchanges are from developed countries to developed countries and not between the economic core and periphery. When national investments are examined, they coincide with exchanges primarily among highly industrialized countries. Canada, Japan, and Western Europe, for example, supply the major sources of foreign investment in the United States. The portion accounted for by other countries actually has been rising, from about 2% in 1970 to 9% in 1988, but the dollar amounts are minimal by comparison. Likewise with American investment abroad: The lion's share (approximately 75%) is to Western Europe, Canada, Japan, and Australia. Over the last 20 years, these percentages have not varied substantially (U.S. Bureau of the Census 1980, pp. 864-65; 1990a, pp. 794, 797). The bulk of international investment, in brief, is within the core rather than the periphery. The recent explosive growth in these transactions signals important qualitative changes in international relations and important changes as well in the likely emergence of hegemonic powers.

All of these indicators suggest pronounced interdependence among economically advanced nations. As business knowledge itself escalates, there is every reason to believe that interdependence will be furthered. Economic interdependence among advanced nations does not necessarily foreshadow an era of harmony and consensus (Chase-Dunn 1987, 1990). But this interdependence should breed similarities and convergence, particularly in economic structure and function. Key economic indicators in economically advanced nations increasingly should resemble one another. Whether this is a function of interdependence, formal economic treaties, or organizational fields—in institutional terms—is not clear. But convergence on key indicators is not in doubt.

Wages are one such indicator. I formerly suggested increasing parity in the wage levels of industrialized nations, with wages in the United States increasingly resembling the levels in other developed nations. Similar movement toward convergence is indicated by another key indicator, levels of productivity. In a study of the 12 member nations of the Organization for Economic Cooperation and Development, the Bureau of Labor Statistics showed that growth in industrial productivity in the United States was less than in four other countries, particularly Japan, but more than in the remaining eight (Dean et al. 1986). Another study of developed nations showed that productivity converged from 1963 to 1982 in 27 of 28 manufacturing industries (Dollar and Wolfe 1988). The same study illustrated that employment mix (as measured by value added per worker) does not explain intercountry differences in productivity.

The distribution of the per capita gross domestic production (GDPs) is becoming more equal in the industrialized nations of the world. Statistics on GDPs are an additional key indicator of convergence. Inequality coefficients in GDPs for this group of nations fell from approximately .15 in 1950 to .02 in 1980, indicating virtual identity in per capita domestic production (Peacock et al. 1988). This is not evidence of hegemony but dramatic testimony to declining differences and declining inequality between highly industrial nations, suggesting a massive redistribution of national incomes and wealth among developed nations. As advances in organizational structure and marketing strategy continue to facilitate expansion into competitive markets, inequality *within* all industrialized countries also should increase—and this in fact is the case (Davis 1992).

The new international economic order thus has exacted a toll on the American economy. The toll reflects the pressures of international competition and the pressures toward a convergent standard of wealth among industrialized nations. Business innovation and knowledge facilitate world trade, world trade breeds interdependence, and this in turn affects the redistribution of wealth among the highly developed nations of the world. As convergence occurs, some nations initially may benefit whereas others may decline. In the 1970s, for example, growth in factory productivity in the United States was only one third that in other developed nations; greater parity was achieved in the 1980s. The declining prices of American goods and escalating inequality in manufacturing are a function of competition among core nations. This decline has little to do with declining productivity in the United States. Rather it is a function of the profound level of interdependence among all economically advanced nations.

In conclusion, I must comment briefly on the concept of productivity so that my argument is perfectly clear. It is true that productivity growth in the United States has not always matched growth in other advanced economies. But discussions of comparative productivity ignore what productivity is and what the dynamics of the international market are about. Productivity is a ratio of output to input. Output is measured by quantity, input by the number of workers employed or the hours they actually work. But in practice, output is difficult to measure over the diversity produced by any economy. Production in apples, oranges, and automobiles cannot be aggregated simply. Therefore, value of shipments is typically substituted for actual physical output. What declining productivity therefore amounts to is not so much increased input producing less output but simply declining worth or value of output on the world market. Declining worth (or prices) for American goods reflects the historical peculiarity of American dominance after World War II, resulting from the battered economies of the Axis and Allies economies, and the loss of monopoly control resulting from the growth in the international economy. American goods are worth less today than in the past, and this fact is simply reflected in productivity data. Lack of dominance in the world market is reflected in declining productivity rather than the other way around.

CONCLUSION

The economies of developed nations expanded dramatically under industrial capitalism. Much growth occurred in the protected environment of a domestic economy with a climate ripe for industrial expansion. But post-industrial capitalism shattered this environment and furnished a new course for economic development. Through novel managerial strategies and organizational innovations, markets broadly expanded into other industrial nations. Competition increased dramatically, shattering the monopoly position many corporations enjoyed in the past.

The discontinuous shift into an intensely competitive international economy suggests the beginnings of a new era in economic trade. In this era, the rise in competition and interdependence encourages wages, as well as productivity, to conform to standards set elsewhere, in other wealthy nations of the world. Some nations, like the United States, dramatically (and traumatically) experienced the initial tugs of convergence in downward pressure on wages and productivity. But in the long run, competition will be similarly felt throughout the industrialized world, with implications for wage levels, standards of living, employment opportunities, and surplus funds available for supporting social welfare.

In summary, the emergence of an international market in the developed world illustrates how economic development advances—swiftly and in a context of increasing competition and increasing inequality. The expansion of international trade consequently generates a sequence of events inconsistent with traditional developmental theory. Developmental theory anticipates the translation of economic growth into higher profits for industry and higher wages for workers. Under industrial capitalism, this principle worked, as core industries distributed the fruits of monopoly power into profits and wages. But under post-industrial capitalism, monopoly power declines and inequality results.

The processes resulting from competition with other core countries, rather than deindustrialization, lagging productivity, or declining hegemony, affect a redistribution of wealth among developed nations and inequality within their domestic economies. Consequently, post-industrial capitalism creates diverse sources of inequality: through expanding personal and retail services and through expanding trade and international competition. Both are fueled by the growth in producer services and the managerial expertise involved in successfully opening new markets. Both feed a national economic profile of dead-end jobs and competitive wage pressure in formerly high-wage sectors.

Whether inequality will continue to escalate depends on several factors, among them whether international competition will diminish as nations move to protect trade from outside intrusion. The critical unknowns at the moment are the European Economic Community and the North American Free Trade Agreement. These organizations could expand domestic markets, but with greater protection from competition by nontreaty members. Particularly important will be the access provided to developing countries in Latin America and to the formerly socialist nations of Eastern Europe. Important too will be comparable treaties fashioned for the burgeoning Asian market, including Indonesia and the People's Republic of China. The hope of politicians is that such treaties will produce long-range efficiencies from short-range difficulties, as Schumpeter (1939) suggested. But at the moment this is unknown.

Also unknown is the economic ability of Second World nations to further intensify international competition. The point has been made that Second World nations were only minimally involved in the trade of highly industrialized nations. But all this can change

easily. Managerial strategies and producer services are skills easily
bought in the market by any corporation with sufficient capital.
Currently, several Second World countries—Mexico, Taiwan, South
Korea, Chile—have the industrial capacity to compete for markets in
the wealthier nations of the world. Rising levels of education will
allow numerous corporations to acquire the managerial resources
necessary to implement competitive strategies. Several of these countries have taken steps to reform their economies so as to encourage
a competitive edge. Evidence suggests both economic development
and substantial growth in select Second World nations (Peacock et
al. 1988). This evidence also suggests that some of the semiperipheral
nations have successfully weathered the economic recessions of recent years (Beenstock 1984). The critical question in all this is the
long-range political stability of developing nations—with the potential for undercutting further economic development.

An additional unknown is the political context of inequality within
developed nations. My focus has been on economic developments
associated with inequality. But other factors shape inequality: governments, classes, unions. These actors affect inequality by influencing
wages and altering the relationships between employees, employers,
and the state. For inequality to advance under post-industrial capitalism, work and politics also must change. In the simplest scenario,
economics influences politics, and tight economic times give way to
political cuts in social services to achieve national efficiency (Okun
1975). But matters are rarely as simple as this. In the following
section, I turn to this subject, with particular emphasis on the management of conflict under post-industrial capitalism.

NOTE

1. *The New York Times.* 1991. "American Revival in Manufacturing Seen in U.S.
Report." February 5, pp. A1 and C17. © *The New York Times;* used with permission.

POLITICS UNDER
POST-INDUSTRIAL CAPITALISM

The economy is crucial for understanding inequality, but the form and substance of its impact are partially regulated in the political arena. Politics consequently plays a key role in inequality. Part of this role is enacted through formal legislation affecting income, wages, taxation, and welfare. Part also involves other political actors including labor unions, voluntary organizations, interest groups, and advocates of one type or another.

In linking politics to inequality, much traditional theory subscribes to an essentially Marxist position. In this view, the economy dominates the institutional order with politics implicated in a subsidiary role. This familiar perspective posits a trade-off between equality and efficiency (Okun 1975). Zukin and DiMaggio (1990), for example, illustrate and paraphrase this view in noting that:

> Workers have been more successful in achieving collective action when the economy produces slack resources that the state can use for side-payments to capital than they have been under conditions of acute fiscal crisis. Under the latter conditions, even workers may be tempted to pursue a narrower and more individualistic form of rationality than would otherwise be the case. (p. 25)

Politics, however, is not just a function of the economy. Although politics may not be wholly independent of class actors, it is more than a simple and direct reflection of economic conditions. The influence of purely political factors may come into play and persist in a variety of economic circumstances.

The political factors implicated in post-industrial capitalism cover the spectrum of managerial alternatives discussed in preceding chapters. Many of these alternatives and innovations have more direct bearing on political manipulation and control than the innovations associated with machine technology and industrial capitalism. Some of these innovations involve the art of persuasion exercised by specialists in the electoral process—as in communications and advertising; others involve more flexible organizations designed to accommodate structural alternatives to traditional labor organizations and union prerogatives; and still others involve the array of managerial strategies to cut costs (and possibly benefits) from social services, including education and health.

In times of economic duress, business groups and corporate alliances are, as Zukin and DiMaggio correctly suggest, more extensively involved in manipulation and political control so as to maintain profits and to effect a competitive advantage. To exercise control, they introduce new resources and innovations into the political arena. Once employed, however, these resources persist as permanent features of the polity—resistant to the vicissitudes of the economy. In this sense, the effects of post-industrial capitalism are not merely or only contingent on the circumstances of economic hardship.

This second section explores two routes to political influence. Chapter 4 considers the factors associated with post-industrial capitalism that are routine extensions of resources available to corporations; these resources heighten social control over adversarial groups regardless of economic circumstances and events. Chapter 5 turns to the topic of privatization to illustrate how politics accommodates deteriorating economic conditions by mixing private-sector development and initiative into the public sector. In both instances, the resources associated with post-industrial capitalism contribute to a more hegemonic political structure favoring business interests and wealthier individuals.

This hegemonic structure erodes class conflict under post-industrial capitalism. Unions decline in importance, working-class politics recedes, and a conservative consensus becomes ever more embracing and pervasive. Hence the paradox of politics and class conflict under post-industrial capitalism: As inequality increases, the potential for militant conflict diminishes among those most affected by economic adversity and circumstance.

Unions, Politics, and
the Frontiers of Social Control

Economic equality has deteriorated rapidly over the last 25 to 30 years. But few politicians or activists have brought this issue to public attention and made it a problem of wider social concern. In fact, commentary on inequality is scant and organized protest absent. The absence of conflict is further reflected in the declining strength of labor, with union membership at an all-time low and labor militancy virtually nonexistent. As for politicians, they are more likely to attend to jobs, economic development, and the plight of the middle class. Inequality is a reality in America today. Economic hardship and adversity are increasingly widespread. But few discuss growing inequality or have championed a movement to address its causes or diminish its effects.

Post-industrial capitalism increases the likelihood that inequality will continue to grow—but in a context of consensus and political tranquility. Labor unions and politics are the traditional vehicles for addressing the problems of inequality. But their passivity is a major irony in America today. Their passivity is also a theoretical anomaly. Many social science theories link inequality to deprivation and conflict. In Marxist theory, protest is a consequence of an increasingly deprived proletariat. But this link between deprivation and protest

diminishes the utility of these theories in explaining the political calm
and the frailty of unions in an era of rising inequality. Thus the
curious blend of economics and politics in contemporary America is
beyond the pale of much traditional social thought. For these theories, America is a paradox and dilemma.

More popular views characterize inequality as a function of cyclical shifts in political power, a pendulum of public opinion and
electoral sentiment cutting an arc along a conservative-liberal axis.
In this view, governments and attitudes change, rather than institutions. The era prior to the 1980s, according to Kevin Phillips (1990),
was seen as a series of costly and ineffectual welfare-state experiments. But the public, in Phillip's view, quickly tired of welfare
politics. Furthermore, international competition brought a message
home to the electorate: Initiate programs to foster competitiveness
rather than dependency. Thus the turn to the conservative ideology
of the right and the entrance of Reagan and Bush.

Reagan unquestionably sharpened the turn to the right and complicated political interests. Although characterized by considerable
rhetoric, Reagan initiated numerous important ideological positions
including a spirited defense of capitalism, individualism, and moral-
ity, as well as an attack on government regulation and intervention.
These positions were more than ideology. His administration placed
this ideology into legislation by decreasing marginal tax rates, accelerating depreciation in business investment, cutting funds for such
programs as the Comprehensive Employment and Training Act
(CETA), and privatizing various government holdings. On top of
this, Reagan's first steps in office, confronting the air controllers and
firing 10,000 controllers point blank, set the tone for more than a
decade of conservative leadership in fashioning a hostile and aggressive attitude toward organized labor (Blumenthal 1986; Himmelstein
1990).

Reagan's mark on conservative politics is beyond dispute. But his
role in turning American politics to the right must be tempered by
several observations, including the most obvious one that inequality
started well before his administration, in the early 1970s. As to union
membership, that too slipped prior to Reagan. Union membership
reached its height in 1950, and, with a single exception, has been
declining ever since. It is, of course, true that Reagan's conservative
views appealed to a broad spectrum of political interests. But so did
the views of Nixon and Eisenhower, each providing landslide victo-

ries for conservative constituencies. In brief, Reagan's role in first initiating and then galvanizing a turn to the right is not all that clear.

In the present chapter I again discuss the use of business rationality to advance corporate interests, but here within the political arena. More than a half century ago, Schumpeter ([1942] 1961) noted the similarities between economic and political resources. In the same way that new resources are available to compete for economic profits, new resources are also available to manage opposition and conflict. These resources are connected to the managerial revolution. They extend to using sophisticated forms of polling, managing and mobilizing opposition, and hiring personnel consultants, public relations specialists, media experts, fund-raisers, advertisers, and others skilled in managing issues strategically.

These resources involve specialized and highly professional talent. Professional resources are costly. They skew access to the very wealthy. These resources consequently are more available to large corporations and business alliances than to labor or the very poor. For this reason the increase in managerial resources in the political arena creates the conditions for political hegemony. Many of these developments have been discussed previously (Clawson and Clawson 1985; Useem 1990). But other implications of post-industrial capitalism and the managerial revolution for politics have been neither well-explored nor fully understood.

First and foremost, managerial resources deserve primacy in the analysis of politics, in addition to the more traditional concerns with rising affluence, the changing electorate, or the impact of international competition. These resources are not only effective in the management of politics but also set a new agenda in political conflict and discourse. The critical issue involves the estimate of these resources as vital to political victory and success. As a consequence of this estimate, these resources are pursued by all factions, including representatives of minorities, the impoverished, and the working class.

But, I shall argue, these resources are pursued at a cost, because their pursuit entails activities inconsistent with strong working-class representation. To use expensive resources, working-class politicians must court and cultivate support from wealthier and more conservative constituents. In this sense, the resources associated with post-industrial capitalism seriously and substantially deprive corporate adversaries of a platform and political voice, but for multiple reasons: because these resources (a) are effective means to advance business interests and (b) must be supported by constituents of ample economic means. This support serves to erode liberal agendas. In this sense, the pursuit of managerial resources establishes a cycle of political abandonment within the circles of working-class politics, by silencing and stifling the very voices certain politicians seek to articulate and represent.

I further argue that these resources are more forceful and influential than coercion and bribery in exercising social control. Playing on sophisticated ideas of value consensus, these resources powerfully affect workers and electorates. Their success suggests that recent developments in sociology, psychology, public opinion, and mass communications provide better understanding and superior means for leverage and influence than the less sophisticated attempts at control present in an earlier era (Griffin et al. 1986). Although satirized in leftist circles as just more of the same thing, these resources accomplished ends that were rarely accomplished with bribery and coercion, as illustrated by two key events: the virtual decimation of the labor movement in American society and the triumph of conservatism across the political spectrum. In the sections that follow, I consider each of these events in turn.

LABOR UNION DECLINE

In 1992, union membership fell to 15.8% of the workforce, the lowest point in more than a half century (U.S. Bureau of the Census 1993, p. 436). The reasons for this decline are open to debate. Many analysts explain this decline by pointing to a deteriorating economy caused principally by international competition. Harrison and Bluestone (1988), for example, talk about business "zapping labor" as a response to America's deteriorating status in the world economy. In their view, union decline is a function of class conflict—but conflict with business triumphant:

> The restructuring process involved more than anything else the abrogation of the social contract that labor, management, and government had slowly but surely constructed in the course of nearly fifty years of union struggle, collective bargaining, and government regulation. . . . By the middle of the 1980s, the broad outlines as well as many of the

> details of these experiments could be summarized in the globalization of production, the hollowing of the firm, outright union busting, and revised labor-management relations that included demands for the lowering of wages, the proliferation of part-time work schedules . . . and the increased subcontracting of work. Together, these developments added up to a realization of the objective—publicly enunciated by a conservative government back at the very beginning of the 1970s—of "zapping labor." (Harrison and Bluestone 1988, p. 51)

According to these authors, deteriorating profits linked to aggressive international competition caused union decline. As profits diminished, as cheap labor from underdeveloped countries became more readily available, employers increasingly were motivated to confront organized labor. And, in Harrison and Bluestone's view, confront them they did—persistently, aggressively, successfully. The pace and tone of this confrontation was set by Reagan's foray into labor relations, setting the hardball pace for conservative politicians and corporate managers in the ensuing decade.

Union decline unquestionably is connected to the aggressive pursuit of business interests. But interpretations stressing the influence of America's deteriorating economic plight are not entirely satisfactory. These interpretations are particularly weak in specifying when and why unions decline. The period of decline is most important. The high point of union membership was reached immediately after World War II. From 1930 to 1945, the percentage of union members in non-agricultural labor tripled, from 11% in 1930 to 35% in 1945 (Kochan, Katz, and McKersie 1986, p. 31). With one exception, a loss followed by a gain in the early 1950s, union strength dropped from the post-World War II height: from 35% in 1945 to 28% in 1965 to 19% in 1985 and less than 16% in 1992 (Kochan, Katz, and McKersie 1986, p. 31; U.S. Bureau of the Census 1990a, p. 419; 1993, p. 436). The brunt of international competition did not fully influence America's economy until the late 1970s and early 1980s. Yet in 1965, union membership had already decreased to 28%, more than one third of a nearly 50-year slide.

Nor do explanations relating to international competition account for the breadth in the erosion in union membership. For example, declining numbers of workers in heavily unionized manufacturing industries, those most at risk from international competition, account for only a small proportion of the decrease in union strength (Dickens and Leonard 1985). Transportation, communications, and utilities, long bastions of union strength, rely heavily on domestic workers and domestic investments. But union decreases were more dramatic there than in manufacturing (Troy 1986). Other service industries, including industries not well-connected to international trade, also show sizable declines (Kochan, Katz, and McKersie 1986). From 1953 to 1985, the percentage of workers unionized in services dropped from 9.5% to 6.6%.

In lieu of searching for a precipitating historical event for union decline among the ravages of international competition, another strategy of explanation may be more useful—an explanation with its premises grounded in at least two salient facts about labor-management relations in the United States. The first fact relates to the lesser role accorded to unions in managing the national economy. In contrast with many of this country's highly unionized international competitors, the United States never approximated a corporatist arrangement. Corporations (and governments) traditionally see unions as an adversary of business rather than as a formal representative of labor's interests. A second fact relates to the effects of labor costs on corporate profits. Although unions sought reforms on several levels, including health and safety, fringe benefits, job security, job definitions, and seniority privileges, the major issue traditionally devolved on wages. Through collective bargaining, unions raised the wages of ordinary workers approximately 10 to 20% higher than nonunionized workers, far more than warranted by the generally higher productivity of union workers (Freeman and Medoff 1984; Lewis 1963). The "sticky" quality of wage raises, especially during recessions, was particularly distasteful to business interests. Labor costs significantly influence profits; Freeman and Medoff show that unionized corporations earn 18% less profit than nonunionized corporations.

Astute managers could not possibly ignore the long-standing influence of unions on corporate profits. As newer resources became available to business, business deployed them in several ways but most specifically to increasingly diminish union presence in the private sector. The resources managers used were those identified with post-industrial capitalism, involving high-level managerial and professional skills rather than the rancorous and confrontational conflict prominent under industrial capitalism. The resources identified with post-industrial capitalism did not guarantee corporate omnipotence, but they did provide a political edge or advantage. And, as previously noted, knowledge-based resources accomplished what politics of previous eras never did so successfully: They considerably diminished the effectiveness of the union movement in America.

Variety in Anti-Union Strategies

Knowledge is neither a panacea for business ills nor the ultimate weapon to advance its aims. Anti-union strategies are more than purely tactical decisions. They involve a contest for the loyalties and allegiances of employees. If programs reliant on knowledge are instituted in pell-mell fashion, behind a cloak of mistrust, with obvious intent to mislead and deceive, then their effects likely will be minimal. Such is the case, I believe, with the multimillion-dollar consultant industry that corporations draw on to mobilize anti-union strategy in accreditation elections (Bureau of National Affairs 1985). The industry employs managerial consultants skilled in communication and public relations. Their tactics vary considerably, but they capitalize on psychological and behavioral approaches to contest union representation. In some instances, these approaches are confrontational and adversarial. In other instances, they may be more sophisticated, involving extensive meetings, communications, small encounter groups—all insinuating the vices and disadvantages of union organization. The tactics capitalize on negative images of the union as demanding high fees and offering little in return.

Confrontational techniques are not terribly effectual in the long run. They play on fear and anxiety rather than consensus and active commitment. Confrontational strategies, even with the aid of managerial consultants, are at odds with what social psychologists know about effective means of persuasion, influence, and commitment. If not instituted as part of an ongoing program of industrial relations—opening up options, opportunities, and elements of free choice for workers—challenges to union representation will be temporary and uneven at best, inconsequential at worst. Confrontation and fear as a basis for motivation simply are unlikely to have lasting and detrimental effects in commitment to a union.

In fact, the evidence on union confrontations, particularly in union elections, is basically inconsistent. In some instances, anti-union specialists increase employer success in union elections and reduce worker support for collective bargaining (Murrimann and Porter 1982). The magnitude of advantage can be substantial (Lawler 1982).

If the approach is illegal, possibly alienating constituent groups, the margin of management success declines (Dickens 1983). In other instances, evidence is more controversial and ambiguous. Lipset (1986) reports research indicating that delaying tactics and unfair labor practices alone do not explain union success in accreditation elections. Lawler (1986) reports several studies illustrating how excessive militancy "boomeranged" and increased support for organized labor. These studies underline the potential impotence of conflict and confrontation.

There is reason to doubt whether managerial consultants are at the root of the continuous decline in union organization since the end of World War II. Although the evidence here is sometimes ambiguous (see, for example, Chaison and Dhavale 1980; Freeman and Medoff 1984), many labor analysts suggest that electoral success is incidental to overall union decline. They suggest, for example, that the climate for growth in union organization is not as encouraging today as in the past; workers today have less faith in the potential of unions to improve their jobs and lot in life (Lipset 1986). Research on management tactics and union defeat in contested elections does not address these important changes in social climate.

Furthermore, even if unions continued to win representation in elections as they did in the mid-1950s, a time of considerable union strength, they would have suffered approximately the same losses they actually experienced (Dickens and Leonard 1985). This projection follows from two important trends in management-labor relations: the declining number of union elections (as a percentage of the labor force) and the declining number of workers involved in these elections (Freeman 1985). Confronting unions in elections, then, may be only one strategy—not a terribly successful one—used by business to phase out union organizations. Something else is occurring that diminishes the importance of organized labor, something more basic to corporate organization and structure. Something other than "bashing" unions is at stake.

My rejection of business militancy to explain union decline neither denies business's antagonism nor ignores managerial abuses, past and present. In the period of industrial capitalism, unions and management struggled intensely and bitterly. Businesses confronted unions head on to undermine their unity and solidarity; intimidation, coercion, police, boycotts, spies, blacklisting, bribes, and the suppression of free speech were all parts of the corporate arsenal (Griffin et al.

1986). The Haymarket violence or the infamous confrontation with Ford symbolized the adversarial stance of management and labor.

Although confrontation and illegal tactics between management and labor continued throughout U.S. history, such methods are less frequent today. They still occur, of course, as indicated by the frequent use of permanent replacement workers—the government's dismissal of the air controllers, and notable actions by firms across the private sector: Greyhound, Boise Cascade, International Paper, and Continental Air, for example. Nonetheless, evidence suggests that confrontational tactics are more likely in the backwaters of the American economy than in the more modernized, high-profit sector with large-scale firms (Foulkes 1980; Kochan 1980).

The New Industrial Relations, 1: Structures and Activities

Developments in personnel management in corporations foreshadow a still different approach to industrial relations. These programs dated back to World War II and its aftermath (Baron et al. 1986). The media labeled them the "new industrial relations" (*Business Week* 1981). This new field made extensive use of professional and managerial consultants experienced in organizational analysis. They shared few of the assumptions of earlier union-management relations. The new industrial relations was developed with little overt conflict and with organizational solutions to corporate problems associated with unions. The programs were phrased in humanistic (and frequently paternalistic) terms, stressing ideals of democracy and labor-management partnerships. Although critics question management's real purpose in instituting these programs, the new industrial relations nonetheless advanced the goals of business more successfully than the previous decades of rancorous conflict and confrontation.

More than a decade ago, *Business Week* (1981) summarized the essentials of the new industrial relations programs by emphasizing

that most people want to be productive and will—given the proper incentives and a climate of labor-management trust—eagerly involve themselves in their jobs. This calls for a participatory process in which workers gain a voice in decision making on the shop floor. Many companies, some in collaboration with once-hostile unions, are creating new mechanisms to gain worker involvement. Among these mechanisms

are "self-managed" work teams, labor-management steering commit-
tees in union shops, problem-solving groups—such as "core groups"
or the quality circles that are widely used in Japan. (p. 85)

Although the details of specific programs vary, the new industrial
programs generally exhibit the trappings of solutions common to
post-industrial capitalism. One key component in these programs is
an altered system of governance involving a more flexible and less
hierarchical structure. In this system, workers play a more important
role in the decisions of the corporation. In some instances, workers
actually own some portion of the business enterprise. In other instances,
workers are consulted on the shop floor regarding production procedures, with the intent of approximating industrial democracy
(Tausky and Chelter 1988). The intent here is to import into the
workplace the ideals of citizenship and democracy, hence compromising market-driven criteria to affect social control.

The new industrial relations also is laden with knowledge contain-
ing social science insights into human motivation and needs. The
needs component reflects a broad organizational view of business as
"natural systems"—with the implication that workers are more than
adjuncts to production. According to Richard Scott (1992), natural
system analysts

emphasize that there is more to organizational structure than the
prescribed rules, the job descriptions, and the associated regularities in
the behavior of participants. Individual participants are never merely
"hired hands" but bring along their heads and hearts: they enter the
organization with individually shaped ideas, expectations, and agendas, and they bring with them differing values, interests, and abilities.
(p. 54)

The new industrial relations plays on the idea of providing workers
with a voice, a feeling of power, and a sense of satisfaction—sentiments usually addressed by unions. The implication here is clear
enough: Increased worker satisfaction would increase productivity,
reduce labor costs, and contribute to more substantial profits
(Gershenfeld 1987; Katz et al. 1983; Norsworthy and Zabala 1985;
Pfeffer and Davis-Blake 1990).

The new industrial relations also relies on extensive managerial
and professional support to implement its goals. Implementation in

turn requires sophisticated conceptions of social influence. Charles Heckscher (1988) refers to this as the "managerialist approach." The managerial approach is primarily a strategy to promote active commitment and involvement of workers throughout the corporation. The strategy plays on the established social psychological principle that influence and control are most firmly established through personal commitment. In this view, value commitments and value consensus become the paramount conduits for social influence—not conflict and coercion, not bureaucratic pressure to conform to externally imposed rules. Consensus is not assumed; it is produced and reinforced through extensive meetings, encounter groups, and quality circles to enhance communication between management and workers. Professionals trained in areas of applied social science are used to implement and advance corporate aims.

The intent of the new relations programs is to provide a new authority structure and a more rational workplace to address the problems and concerns of management. Some of these problems are economic and relate to wages extending beyond productivity to the point of eroding corporate profits (Freeman and Medoff 1984). Other problems relate to union work rules designed to protect employee rights. Managers complain that innovations in marketing and technology produce more specialized product lines, shorter product life cycles, and greater need for flexibility in work arrangements. But obligatory union rules defining job classifications and priorities may be too rigid for innovations in job definitions and computer-based production and for the general revolution in work associated with the "second industrial divide" (Piore and Sabel 1984). Still other problems relate to productivity and reflect an underlying suspicion that American management prematurely abandoned human relations, that satisfaction heightens productivity, and that economic success in other countries is connected to greater awareness of worker needs (Farber 1987; Hull and Azumi 1988; Osterman 1988).

The multiple intentions of this corporate agenda suggest numerous ambiguities in the phrasing and implementation of the new industrial relations. In part, the programs mouthed the methodology of a human relations perspective involving informal relations, participation, decision making, cooperation, autonomy and trust—always with a view toward minimizing bureaucracy, hierarchy, and authority. But these programs also were cast not primarily to advance a humanistic workplace but more usually to undermine union initiatives and union presence and to increase corporate profits. These programs always made different assumptions than collective bargaining would, highlighting the psychological needs of workers rather than their economic priorities. There was no attempt to weave together union and management demands, reflective of former programs in industrial relations. Unions were bypassed to effect direct communication with workers. Always the intention was to keep unions at bay. Consequently, the new industrial relations programs attempted a multiple strategy to put in place structural alternatives to unions, without, of course, the presence of the union itself. The question remains, however, as to what these programs accomplished and how effective they were.

The New Industrial Relations, 2: Consequences and Implications

Variants on the new industrial relations are long-standing in American industry. By 1980, on the eve of Reagan's election to the presidency, some form of the new industrial relations was widespread, touching at least one third of the workforce. Almost one quarter of all employees reported participating in such programs, with the proportion increasing to two thirds in the very largest firms (Kochan, Katz, and McKersie 1986). The presence of these programs also was dramatically higher in the fastest growing and most profitable industries (Kochan and Cappelli 1984). In brief, some form of new industrial program already was in force before the 1980s.

Are new industrial relations programs successful? No single answer is sufficient to respond to this question. On the one hand, these initiatives are more programmatic and less confrontational than the use of managerial consultants during union elections. At the same time, these programs are ripe with ambiguity and contradiction, weaving together advanced principles of influence with interesting and idealized estimates of individual needs and placing the composite over a base of distinctly anti-union sentiments. Not coincidentally, these programs succeed in some instances and fail in others, although there is much more here than meets the eye.

First, the obvious and the negative. In terms of satisfaction and productivity, the record of these programs is uneven at best, dismal at worst. Consider the following case in point: the introduction of "enlightened management" into the Johnson & Johnson medical supply plant in Albuquerque, New Mexico. In a fiery indictment of managerial motivation, Guillermo Grenier (1988) details the oppressive rigor and authoritarian control associated with the new industrial relations. Johnson & Johnson projected an image of responsible management, an image in keeping with its rank in *Fortune* as the third most respected employer in America. The personnel system was organized to treat workers as knowledgeable, to enhance a sense of community, and to heighten worker control. Quality circles rallied worker sentiments in promising interesting jobs, employee growth and development, and worker dignity. The byword was managerial humanism. The company portrayed managers as fair and responsive. Workers and managers were partners and allies, capable of relating to one another without recourse to a third party. When a union did try to organize the plant, a managerial consultant was invited in and the union was defeated.

The practices associated with this example of new industrial relations suggest several interesting, if dehumanizing, innovations in labor relations. First, quality circles are sophisticated encounter groups. Problems are "psychologized." The worker is the patient. Problems are said to reside in the patient, not in the corporation. The circles try to mold personality and increase worker conformity to managerial demands. Union advocates are not merely identified but are cast as deviants and threats to plant stability. Second, managers are extraordinarily sophisticated. Information and communication are handled with skill and finesse. But information also is used deviously: to weaken worker solidarity, to enhance managerial legitimacy, and to increase surveillance, all with a view toward raising productivity and profit (Fantasia et al. 1988; Grenier and Hogler 1991). At the same time, the largely female and Hispanic workers at the Johnson & Johnson plant were generally content with their jobs. They enjoyed extraordinary fringe benefits, particularly health insurance and generous maternity leaves.

Grenier's critique of the new industrial relations is valid in some instances. Behind the cloak of democracy and humanitarian relations, management was authoritarian in methods and intent. But an across-the-board indictment of the new industrial relations is questionable. These programs try to motivate workers rather than intimidate them. Are these effects achieved? Again, the record is uneven. Kochan, Katz, and McKersie's (1986) landmark study suggests minimal influence of the new industrial relations on productivity and labor costs. They conclude by suggesting that the trust implied in the new industrial relations, the commitment to worker integrity and autonomy, will have to diffuse throughout the corporate structure—from shop floor to board room—for these programs to work effectively. American workers suspect management; in numerous instances, this suspicion has just cause. Consequently, management may not be able simply to import the "Japanese model" without dramatically changing its treatment of and attitude toward workers (Hull and Azumi 1988).

The new industrial relations has questionable influence on productivity and satisfaction, but the impact is significant in another important respect. The highly psychologized approach to industrial relations, replete with the full array of personnel managers, human resource departments, and sensitivity training groups, forms an emergent foundation for a structural alternative to unions. The mere presence of these programs in some form gives many workers both voice and power. Wherever these programs have been initiated, unions experienced difficulty in securing a stronghold: "Taken together, these new company human resource policies, plus new legal regulations . . . have given many workers most of the benefits and protections commonly provided by unionization. . . . Their net impact has been to make union organizing more difficult" (Strauss 1984, p. 5).

Numerous studies corroborate the link between the new industrial programs and ineffectual union organization. Firms with enlightened labor policies—policies that address human relations-type questions—were more successful in reducing union membership in both new and existing work facilities. Research indicates that the following types of policies, all reflecting commitment to the procedures of the new industrial relations, decrease the potential for successful union organization:

Grievance systems
Worker participation programs
Work-sharing arrangements
Pay-for-knowledge
Salaried pay schedules
Production discussions
Opportunities for worker-management communication (Cappelli and
    Chalykoff 1986; Fiorito et al. 1987; Kochan, McKersie, and Chalykoff
    1986)

These programs affect union failure in elections independently of one another or pose other obstacles to accreditation elections or to initiating collective bargaining.

This research also suggests that industrial relations programs generally succeed in defeating unions regardless of management's orientation toward labor—whether managers are positive or negative toward unionization. The programs thus do not simply reflect managerial policy. Although the programs may not increase satisfaction or productivity, they lead workers to consider unions as incidental. The new industrial relations is consequently much more than old wine in new bottles. In this sense, whether it represents a decided shift in management or merely window dressing, as Grenier and other skeptics note, is important but not the vital issue. What is vital are the effects of the system as much as the motivations of a corporate elite. And the effects of the new industrial relations are clear in accomplishing what older confrontations were never able to do successfully: check the pace of union growth and dramatically reverse its course. Managerial control is at new heights and new levels of sophistication.

The decline in unions is in no sense benign. It is the purposeful aim of industrial programs. These programs are the core of a wider strategy by business to diminish the presence of organized labor. Research on investment in unionized plants and on union elections in new plants suggests that the union system (at least in the competitive private sector) may be in a state of devolution as a consequence of corporate investment and planning. Kochan, Katz, and McKersie (1986, pp. 72-73) indicate that management invests less capital in unionized than in nonunionized plants. New plants with innovations in industrial relations are less likely to be unionized (Fiorito et al. 1987). Also, not all new plants opening in recent years have union elections; and among those that do, few workers, about 20% of the total, vote in favor of unions. I do not intend to minimize the strident policy whereby businesses fight unions tooth and nail. But I do suggest that the union system in private industry is in decline—and not because of overt and rancorous conflict. Management has strategically and deliberately planned for the demise of unionized labor, drawing on the extensive resources associated with human relations and personnel management systems. A new structure is taking the place of unions, particularly in the large corporations able to afford the considerable costs associated with administering programs in industrial relations (Cornfield 1986).

The new industrial relations is part and parcel of the broad array of developments associated with post-industrial capitalism, including a partial devolution of authority, a broad attempt to rationalize control by using general social science knowledge, and an increased use of professional specialization in personnel management. These resources, furthermore, are effectual—more so than the conflict and confrontation present in the past. In this sense, post-industrial capitalism erodes union strength. This, then, is its contribution to labor-management relations: undermining effective unionization at a time of deteriorating standards of inequality. Consequently the irony: Low-wage jobs proliferate with organized labor unable to intervene.

WORKING-CLASS POLITICS
UNDER POST-INDUSTRIAL CAPITALISM

Since the end of World War II, a pro-business consensus has pervaded American politics. The consensus joins free-market ideology to traditional liberal thought, reflecting what Alan Wolfe (1977) has called the "new Democratic" policy. The ideological content of this consensus stipulates that business interests best serve society by prevailing over the interests of the poor. Resources are primarily for economic growth and development. The core of a good society is a healthy economy with a proper climate for business. The influential McKinsey Global Institute, with a star-studded board of distinguished economists on its roster, concluded that this climate is by far the most important advantage of America in global competition (*New York Times* 1992f). This climate and the commitment to a healthy economy do not preclude support for social welfare. Their ascendance does mean, however, that the lion's share of resources is earmarked for business goals.

The indicators of this consensus are everywhere:

- Presidential involvement in corporate negotiations, under the guise of securing needed jobs
- Growing tolerance for heightened unemployment (over inflation)
- Increased experimentation with welfare—usually involving the severance of payments
- Growing homelessness (and growing tolerance of the problem)
- Major downsizing efforts in large corporations

Although all of these activities can be defended on other grounds, they add up to an increasingly pro-business environment, a conservative accord. This pro-business environment suggests a market renaissance reflecting the increased importance of supply and demand for resolving social and economic issues and a diminishing role for government, as in socialism or mixed economies (Polanyi 1957).

Although Reagan sharpened the edge of conservative politics by initiating a wholesale defense of capitalism, rugged individualism, and free-market economics, the conservative consensus began well prior to the Reagan administration. In one form or another, Democrats and Republicans alike have shared this view, going back at least to Eisenhower and extending through the administrations of Carter, Nixon, Kennedy, Ford, Bush, and Clinton. Johnson's extensive War on Poverty may be one of the few examples departing somewhat from a staunch conservative stance.

Why did this consensus surface? On this there is much less agreement. Traditional theory speaks of a decline in working-class conflict. Seymour Lipset (1968), for example, discusses the "democratization of the class struggle," whereas Clark Kerr and his colleagues (1964, p. 209) note growth in an "industrial relations system for establishing and administering the rules of the workplace" and replacing violent and explosive outbursts. Numerous observers suggest that class voting is decreasing, both in the United States and in Western Europe. Ronald Inglehart (1984, 1986) interprets this decline as reflecting a shift from a materialist to a postmaterialist axis; with affluence, class concerns diminish. Other writers observe that classes retain distinct political interests, although their salience reflects both the political climate and the severity of economic times (Eulau and Lewis-Beck 1985). Nonetheless, it is reasonable to conclude that the links between working-class constituencies, liberal politics, and welfare legislation have broken down in the United States, scattering issues and commitments across the political spectrum. The older rules dividing the political spectrum into clusters of poor, liberal Democrats and rich, conservative Republicans no longer have much validity (Wolfe 1987).

The move to a conservative consensus jeopardizes political solutions to economic disparities. It weakens the ability of politics to address growing inequality. Because welfare benefits with their many warts, drawbacks, and vices substantially diminish inequality, this topic is important for understanding post-industrial capitalism (Reynolds and Smolensky 1977). The consensus moves America further to the

right than in the past—and further to the right of most other industrialized nations—in permitting corporations to alter the conditions
of employment. But the arguments on class politics summarized
above offer only partial insight into how this consensus came about.
Few arguments confront the anomaly of declining class politics in a
context of recent escalation in economic inequality. In many instances, the presuppositions in these arguments are open to question,
as in the changing voting behavior of the electorate. Ignored, for
example, is the possibility of a shifting structure of electoral politics
and how structural shifts might diminish electoral support for a
liberal agenda. Ignored also is the possibility that interests may be
more or less stable, with change primarily affected by the altered
resource base of the political structure (McCarthy and Zald 1977).

My position parallels the argument previously advanced about
unionization: that knowledge-based resources effectively diminish
the power of adversaries and neutralize their influence. But this
argument is more complex than the previous one in two respects.
First, unlike the situation with unions, business has no legal control
over the political context in a way comparable to its legal control over
the workplace. Accordingly, influence must be more indirect and
also used within the confines established by someone else, in this
instance the state. Second, the political arena is itself complex, trav-
ersing at least two important, although related, domains: relationships with the state and its regulatory agencies and relationships
with political parties in the electoral process. In this section, I will
attempt to show how some of the unique characteristics of knowledge-
based resources did for working-class politics what they did for
unions: diminished the prospects for mounting a successful campaign against business interests.

The Changing Political Resources of Business

Recent interpretations of declining working-class politics point to
a line of inquiry with an emphasis different than voting. In this work,
analysts direct attention to the massive mobilization of business
interests and to the victory of these interests over labor, the working
class, and other traditional adversaries. Political scientists refer to
this as the "advocacy explosion," that is, as an expansion in the
organizations lobbying for special interests. The expansion reflects
the increased availability of professionals and managers, increased

attention to the social and political environment, particularly relations with the state, and the expanded technical knowledge base
necessary for influencing outcomes related to business goals. These
are the resources and concerns associated with post-industrial capitalism; they supplement motivation and enhance political influence.
These resources do not guarantee dominance, but they provide an
edge in the adversarial relations between the more and less fortunate.

The professional representation of business interests has broad-
ened dramatically in national politics. More than a decade ago,
analysts started to document the magnitude of these interests. Writing during Reagan's first year in office, Robert Reich (1981) pointed
to the massive numbers of personnel already in place to negotiate
business-government relations: 12,000 Washington lawyers, 9,000
lobbyists, 42,000 trade association personnel, 8,000 public relations
specialists, 1,300 public affairs consultants, 1,200 specialized journal-
ists, and 3,500 business affairs consultants. In discussing these workers, Reich (1981) notes that

> this group possesses such unusual skills and represents so particular
> an economic interest that it seems fair to refer to them as an industry
> unto themselves—an industry that is growing rapidly in an environ-
> ment that it has done much to create. (p. 84)

The influence of business in governmental affairs has been considerable since the founding of this country. But evidence suggests that
business representation and influence are not only growing rapidly,
but at a pace more rapid than other interests. In this sense, the
advocacy explosion is less an across-the-board eruption of representation than an increasingly advantaged edge skewed to the corporation. Looking at a cross-section of political interest groups,
Schlozman (1984) showed that business presence in Washington
increased from 57% in the 1970s to 72% in the 1980s (Schlozman and
Tierney 1983; Yoffie 1987). Using a broader definition—with presence in Washington defined as having an office, counsel, or consultant there—then 86% of all the organizations in Schlozman's study
represented business interests. The percentages representing labor,
civil rights groups, and advocates for environmental reform were
minuscule by comparison. Not surprising is labor's diminished role
in Washington politics. Not surprising either are the interests most
represented—the giants of industry with dominant positions in their

market (Jacobs et al. 1991). These are the firms with the capital needed to support a professional and increasingly costly source of influence. Access to these resources clearly shifts power away from the electorate and further undermines the politics of pluralism.

Some writers interpret this increase in business representation as a new stage of capitalism. Useem (1990), for example, sees this representation as suggesting the emergence of "institutional capitalism"; this results from an increasing identity of interests concentrated in the corporate sector. Corporations, in Useem's view, are more sensitive now than in the past to general business interests and are more likely to advance policies reflecting class-wide benefits. Others interpret this representation as a proactive stand in reply to the increased powerlessness business interests experience. These authors point to a growing litany of business complaints:

Declining profits among American firms

The strangulation of business by a state more committed to welfare than capital growth

The intrusion of regulatory agencies into the free market

The exhaustion of liberal programs and experiments

Threats from global competition (Akard 1992; Clawson and Clawson 1985; Harrison and Bluestone 1988; Phillips 1990; Silk and Vogel 1976; Useem 1990)

The expansion of business interests is consistent on several counts with my position on post-industrial capitalism. Most basically, the supply of resources must be underscored. Representation of this magnitude was simply impossible in the largely manufacturing and agricultural society of 75 years ago. Increased education, increased specialization in psychology, sociology, and business, and an increased service sector are the foundation for such extensive representation (Walker 1983).

Also, the extension of business representation is not just an extension of influence but an extension drawing on the knowledge associated with post-industrial capitalism. The very same skills used to command the economic arena are used in politics as well. To illustrate, a sample of corporate officers from *Fortune* 500 companies indicated in interviews that public relations departments were different than in the past, that they were more than lobbying efforts involving the use of raw pressure to secure political advantage

(Baysinger and Woodman 1982). Political representation, for example, was more professional and involved considerable technical expertise. Influence occurred at political hearings. The arguments of lobbyists were technically complicated, requiring information, research findings, and detailed legal briefs (Schlozman and Tierney 1983). Representation is consequently consistent with the format of post-industrial capitalism, drawing on knowledge, professionals, and advanced specialization. Out of style are the parties, bribes, glad hands and under-the-table favors of a former era (Hofstadter 1973). These estimates concur with Laumann and Heinz's (1985) comments on the functions of the Washington lawyer:

> Raw influence peddling was generally seen to be very much the exception. Effective representation . . . required careful and exhaustive preparation of the case, with high-quality information and documentation being provided to the decision makers. . . . Being a "glad-hander," appearing on the cocktail party circuit . . . were seen as marginal tactics. (p. 495)

The firms involved in the diffusion of business influence resemble the producer services used by corporations for furthering market strategies. Representatives for business interests are employed in firms with across-the-board expertise in law, politics, advertising, and public relations. Corporations employ these firms both as sources of advice for managing internal activities and increasingly for attending to their external and political interests. In their analysis of the Washington lawyer, Laumann and Heinz (1985, p. 501) note the increase in "one-stop shopping for a growing number of corporate clients who need legal, lobbying and public relations help." Also, as Reich (1981) correctly notes, the massive lobbying effort initiated by business takes on a momentum of its own. These firms are entrepreneurial, seeking out new associations and new business to add on to existing activities.

The expanding representation of interests is integral to the way large corporations now function. This representation is decidedly not an afterthought, a fad in the profile of business. Businesses, of course, always paid attention to the political environment through trade associations, chambers of commerce, or the American Association of Manufacturers, for example. But under post-industrial capitalism, such attention is more extensive, more systematic, more routinized, and built into the very foundations of the firm's organizational chart. The external concerns of business increasingly are lodged in a departmental office. The departments expend organizational time and energy and require full-time staffs to administer. More than one half of *Business Week's* list of 1,000 large corporations had public affairs units (Post et al. 1983). A study of *Fortune* 500 corporations suggested similar conclusions: About 80% had a department dedicated to government relations or public affairs (Baysinger and Woodman 1982). In addition, corporations increasingly emphasize the political skills of management, to assure that power and political knowledge are consolidated (Useem 1985, p. 15).

The growing resource base of American capitalism and its extension into the lobbies of government goes some way in explaining an increasingly conservative consensus in national politics (Clawson and Clawson 1985; Mizruchi 1992; Useem 1990). Yet, convincing as these indications of business hegemony may be, there is something missing here, something omitted in fully explaining an emergent conservative consensus. Specifically, these materials on representational interests are incomplete in inadequately accounting for political opposition. By looking at corporations, their expanding resources, and their influence, much attention is directed toward managers and little to the issue of class relations. Is the implication of this mobilization that managers are omnipotent because of their proximity to capital resources and representational interests? In Friedland and Alford's (1991, pp. 241-42) terms, managerial-based theories overstate influence by assuming that elites "have extraordinary latitude to make strategic choices determined only by their access to material resources." What is needed is further analysis of competition as discussed in reference to the economy—but rephrased for an analysis of class relations. What role, if any, do working-class advocates play in structuring the conservative consensus? This is another part of the emerging conservative consensus and another part of what business resources are about.

Unanticipated Consequences of Business Mobilization

Traditional explanations of the conservative consensus discuss how the power and influence of business reduce the legitimacy of opponents, weaken the position of labor and the working class, and fashion a hegemonic defense of business interests (Cooper and Soley

1990; Pescheck 1987; Sabato 1981, 1984). An additional option to explain the conservative consensus holds that working-class opposition and ideology persist, but labor's voice and platform have been undermined. This latter option should be briefly explored, and to do so, it is necessary to reexamine a key concept in post-industrial capitalism: what knowledge-based resources are about.

Knowledge-based resources are more than alternative options for social actors. A basic premise in my argument concerning post-industrial capitalism is that they are frequently better options than what went on before them—more influential than conflict, more on target than whim, fad, or fashion. Knowledge-based resources are progressively superior means of rationalizing action. This suggests that once these resources are available and deployed, they render older ways of acting obsolete. Although anyone can draw on older ways of effecting social and economic goals, they do so at peril and risk if all others in a situation are using more advanced and resourceful techniques.

The progression implied in these resources suggests that once used, they alter the institutional context and change the way competitors must act, if they are at all interested in besting their adversaries. Such is the case with the electoral process and how it is conducted. In the same way that professional and knowledge-based resources have flooded the public affairs departments and the lobbying efforts of corporations, so have managerial skills and professional expertise come to roost in the electoral process. I refer specifically to the entry of professionals to politics, professionals capable of focusing elections; managing, defining, and refining issues; estimating public opinion; and mobilizing sentiments. The professionals are pollsters, advertisers, public relations firms, focus groups, and media experts specializing in elections. As with other examples of expertise under post-industrial capitalism, election specialists have no magic. They cannot turn elections around if there is nothing to turn. But they can provide an edge, particularly important in close races.

This growing resource base of election professionals, one of the key foundations in politics under post-industrial capitalism, has dramatically altered electoral activities in America. Once deployed by one competitor, knowledge-based resources must be deployed by all others. If one party uses television advertising, the other must follow suit. If one uses polling techniques to sort out the preferences of the electorate, the other must likewise do this or at least be aware of the options. This means that electoral politics today increasingly are dominated by elites, professionals, and more organized interests (Edsall 1984). Their contribution parallels the contribution of producer services to business: to expertly gauge demand, direct it to advantage, market candidates, and in turn generate other critical resources, notably legitimacy and campaign funds. Edsall (1989) discusses this as a "shift toward a political system dominated by technology—a highly sophisticated mix of detailed polling, focus groups, targeted direct mail, and television and radio commercials precisely tailored in response to the flood of information concerning public attitudes" (p. 279). He goes on to note that

> the shift to expensive technology, in turn, elevated fund-raising from a critically important factor in campaigns, to the dominant factor. The sharp escalation of the importance of money gave the Republican Party a decided advantage over the Democratic Party. Campaign contributors are overwhelmingly concentrated among the upper-middle class and the rich, just the groups among whom Republican allegiance is strongest. (pp. 279-80)

The movement to more knowledge-infused techniques of marketing and persuasion suggests that superior resources and funding may have tipped the electoral balance in favor of centrist causes and liaisons with wealthier individuals and interests. It means also that the older bases of representation may have changed and changed hands. The interest groups of the past are either not represented or represented differently. The movement suggests why political parties and groups increasingly abandon the impoverished, the minorities, the homeless, and the deprived: These groups cannot provide the contributions and donations necessary to sustain new and advanced electoral technology.

Voting patterns change, according to this view, not because the political attitudes of the poor are altered or turned to the right, but because political managers abandon the poor in a search of wealthy constituents to support costly election technology. Thus, to return to a former point on class-based voting, the decline in class voting may be more than meets the eye. The failure to support liberal positions, for example, may not in reality reflect the erosion in traditional class values. Conceivably, liberal ideals run strong in the working class but cannot surface in local and national elections. Just this possibility is suggested in Himmelstein and McRae's (1988) analysis of data on public opinion:

The direct relationship between SES and conservatism on the pivotal economic issue of domestic spending still appears to be quite alive; conservatism . . . is directly related to income, class, and occupational status. . . . If the relationship between SES and conservatism is not inverse . . . the development of postmaterialist values cannot explain the decay of the traditional socioeconomic bases of political party allegiance. (p. 506)

Ferguson and Rogers (1986) similarly suggest that traditional leftist views have not eroded—even on the eve of Reagan's 1980 victory. In the decade immediately prior to Reagan's election, they find no significant turn to the center or right:

On the issue of whether there was too much power in the hands of a few large companies, about 61% of respondents said that there was, compared to 79% in 1979.

On the issue of whether business was making excess profit, 31% agreed in 1969, as opposed to 51% in 1979.

On whether government should limit profits, 33% said yes in 1969 versus 60% in 1979.

Nor do Ferguson and Rogers feel that Reagan's charisma distorted class allegiance, because his popularity was not dramatically different from Johnson's, Nixon's, Ford's, or Carter's. They conclude that interest groups, not voters, have realigned their interests. In brief, these authors question the central premise in research on class voting: That shifting differences reflect alterations in class values. They argue that shifting differences among voters are less important than the shifting interests of political elites.

A double-barreled advantage consequently is associated with increasing corporate influence under post-industrial capitalism: (a) greater resources dedicated to business interests flooding the political arena with (b) changing electoral processes favoring solicitations from wealthier constituents. This effect, hinted at by Przeworski (1985) in another context, is about how the destiny of leftist politics is fashioned by the support required for garnering important resources—not numerical majorities but money and electoral technology. This argument also resembles the popular claim that politicians must use entitlement rights rather than working-class welfare to court the vote of middle-class majorities.

The costs and increases in these resources suggest a simple truism of American politics today: The poor are underrepresented. They are less likely to be courted, have less to contribute financially, and, as a result, are less likely to participate in politics. But, as illustrated in previous chapters, they are, and will continue to be, a presence in the American economy. Not coincidentally, voter turnout from the lower strata dropped precipitously during the 1960s and 1970s, when much of this apparatus was put in place (Cavanaugh 1981). Class voting consequently declines in part because the poor are not on the political agenda. If not nurtured and reinforced, liberal beliefs may wither or succumb to the conservative appeal. Electoral politics short-circuits representation of the poor, thus allowing inequality to increase and be ignored in the arena of national politics.

CONCLUSION

The simultaneous rise in inequality and the declining opportunity to do much about it is a telling irony in America today. It is also an anomaly in the context of sociological theory. Radical and liberal theory rotate on an ideological pivot of progress. Forces develop in opposition to vested interests. Conflict prevails. But does it? Are reactions to injustice inevitable? Many Marxists respond affirm-atively. But social life has no built-in equilibrium; no normalcy, no fulcrum, no center of gravity pulls political attention and reaction toward a solution to economic inequities. Reactions do not just materialize. Social and political movements are required to mobilize resources, to draw attention to social concerns, and to rectify the problems involved.

Post-industrial capitalism directs more attention than radical and liberal theories to the newer resources available for furthering busi-ness interests—as well as to the possibility of diminishing the pres-ence of adversarial groups. Post-industrial capitalism theory also suggests that today businesses are more concerned with their politi-cal environment and cope with the environment more effectively than in the past. Adversarial organizations such as labor unions may be managed, diminished in strength, or replaced by others more sympathetic to the aims of management. The theory of post-industrial capitalism assumes nothing about progress or about the predilection of the disadvantaged to inherit anything.

The decline in the left strengthens centrist political power and solutions. The signs are everywhere: new and growing respect for free markets, the abandonment of New Deal objectives, the proliferation of conservative think tanks, the surfeit of conservative media experts, the more conservative views of elected officials and court appointees (Clawson and Clawson 1985; Cooper and Soley 1990; Pescheck 1987). The media refer to these trends as Reagan's legacy, but that view misses the more deep-rooted base for a centrist consensus in American society. The organization, management, and resources of business interests suggest that trends toward conservatism are more than the ups and downs of business and political cycles.

A resurgence of liberalism is always possible. But my analysis suggests that were a resurgence to occur, it would be substantially closer to the center or right than in days gone by. America is consequently in a unique position in the global economy, with increasingly lower levels of unionization than its important trading powers (notably Germany and Japan) and an increasingly diminished welfare net of social benefits. Paul Krugman (1994) has written that countries do not compete, that they have no well-defined bottom lines and are not at risk of going out of business. But they may act as if they are in business.

I suspect that the arguments formulated by new generations of managers and professionals in business increasingly convince an ever wider public that the U.S. government ought to provide the political infrastructure of a pro-business economy. This opens up a possibility that behind the facade of free-market ideology, a corporatist America is emerging from the past, with governments increasingly calling on business for managerial expertise and in turn providing new resources and new opportunities for profit. In the next chapter, I turn to one case illustrating how this might happen, how it involves post-industrial capitalism and what it will mean for social and economic inequality.

The Privatization of Welfare
and the Triumph of the Market

In the 1980s, the Reagan administration popularized privatization as an alternative to big government. His administration targeted 11,000 government activities that could be more cheaply and efficiently owned and operated by the private sector. At that time, the private sector already administered substantial proportions of welfare, with some jurisdictions showing nearly one half of all welfare controlled by private business (Hasenfeld 1984). Some of these services were routine activities such as clerical assistance or the delivery of meals to the elderly. But other activities were core welfare services managed by big businesses. The market in welfare is large and lucrative, ripe with opportunity for private-sector development. Informed forecasts suggest that publicly supported social service programs would continue to be maintained but increasingly over a grid of market economic principles (Gilbert 1983).

Privatization uses the free market as a model for organizing welfare. The philosophy underlying privatization reexamines the distinction between the public and private sector. Privatization advocates recommend the expansion of the market not geographically but into the public domain, into the institutional arenas of welfare, health, and education. The intent is to skew the mix of private, nonprofit, and public sectors in welfare to a new set richer in private presence and alternatives. This intent reflects the increased esteem accorded the market, contributing to its stature as a basis for emulation, a model for the way everyday affairs should be organized.

Privatization brings to education and health the same criteria used in business: efficiency, productivity, profitability, and cost. Privatization proposals emphasize the importance of competitive procedures in enhancing the quality and reducing the costs of welfare. These proposals use all of the resources associated with post-industrial capitalism, including cost-benefit analyses, marketing, and advertising. The proposals assume that the broad spectrum of business rationality—as well as the know-how, the common sense, and the savvy of business—can provide a superior product at reduced costs. Privatization is an alternate way business professionals and managers increase their presence in an industry, gain power over organizational resources, and implement procedures to rationalize services and increase competition, sales, and profits.

Privatization has a long history, dating back at least to Bentham's ([1789] 1948) recommendations on prisons. In recent years, privatization proposals range from Charles Whittle's Edison Project (financed by Time-Warner) to health care regulated by "managed competition"—as suggested most recently by the Clinton administration. Many of the welfare activities targeted for privatization are already highly rationalized (Starr 1982). Nursing homes, day care, and medical care are all multimillion-dollar businesses. Investors buy and sell shares on the stock exchange, subjecting welfare to pressures for increasing profit. Furthermore, private welfare services show the same trend toward large size and concentration as commercialized, business enterprises (Stoesz 1986). Beverly Enterprises, Kinder-Care, and Humana are big businesses. Privatization is a sure-fire agenda for this trend toward growth to continue and for rationalization to increasingly diffuse throughout the welfare sector.

Because privatized social services are modeled after business organizations, privatization is a textbook case for studying institutional emulation—the processes by which one sector takes on the procedures and trappings of another (DiMaggio and Powell 1983; Meyer and Rowan 1977). But it is a case with a twist. In most illustrations of emulation, sectors are within a single institutional domain. Here they traverse an institutional divide, diffusing from a business sector concerned with private profit into a welfare sector concerned with social need. In this chapter, I question whether the market model can be generalized across the institutional spectrum. Specifically, I consider whether the technological inventories, the procedures associated with post-industrial capitalism, can use the competitive market to lower the costs associated with welfare and still deliver high-quality services equitably and efficiently.

Privatization advocates radiate confidence about converting social services into privatized businesses. But this conversion is by no means straightforward. Doubts stem from the divergent norms and tasks associated with welfare and business. Each is structured according to dissimilar and conflicting logics. My argument is that this divergence limits the potential for managerial strategies to meet the multiple demands involved in reducing costs and at the same time sustain the guarantees of equity and quality commonly associated with citizenship. I will show how these divergences result in a costly and inefficient system of privatized welfare and, furthermore, how the inefficiencies under privatization are typically unnoticed, not because of neglect or pattern evasion but because the checks on quality and efficiency built into the system presume a level of knowledge and expertise not easily accessible to either social planners or welfare consumers.

Privatization, in brief, encourages the establishment of a partially dysfunctional system of social welfare. Were this system to flourish, the likely outcome would be a two-tiered structure: private access for the advantaged who chose to circumvent the defects of privatization, and privatization for the disadvantaged, those deprived of other alternatives. Thus, privatization further illustrates how managerial strategies and increased competition result in heightened inequality. As the economy increases in importance and stature—a model to be admired and emulated—welfare and business are joined. The inequalities associated with business and the economy then become ever more pervasive, spreading into the distribution of welfare itself.

ECONOMIC CHANGE AND
THE FUTURE OF SOCIAL WELFARE

Current interest in privatization unfolds in a climate increasingly disposed toward market solutions. This climate is nurtured by the economic difficulties from global competition and the stark realities of diminishing productivity and of profitability at risk. In the United

States, the slack funds previously available for welfare are increasingly scarce. But even in major welfare states, including Sweden and the Netherlands, financial difficulties press the declining national surpluses used to underwrite welfare costs.

At the same time liberal constituencies in the United States are declining in importance and are increasingly incapable of shoring up support for social welfare. Conservatives, on the other hand, identify welfare with socialism, the handout, the dole. After all, conservative ideologues argue, the billions of dollars invested in public welfare did little to diminish poverty, reverse declining educational achievement, or eradicate a growing underclass in the American class structure. Public opinion polls continue to show increased distrust of Americans toward government and politicians (Lipset and Schneider 1987). Overt and aggressive resentment and distrust of government have surfaced in countless recent elections, including the unusual support for a third-party candidate for president in 1992—with a platform subscribing to the limitations of government as a panacea for America's ills and adhering to the overriding conviction that government was (and could be run as) just another business. A generation ago Daniel Bell (1973, pp. 41-42) wrote that post-industrial society will see the establishment of "broader social criteria" at the cost of production and other noneconomic values. But there is no indication that this vision will materialize.

A long-standing aversion to socialism in the United States accentuates the conservative consensus, making welfare more vulnerable to harsh economic winds. Americans are fascinated with market-based solutions. This fascination reflects a deep-seated view that business and the market are more efficient than politicians and bureaucrats. As Lane (1986) notes,

> the public tends to believe that the market system is a more fair agent than the political system. People . . . ignore many of the public benefits and, with certain exceptions, prefer market goods to political goods. They prefer the market's criteria of earned deserts to the polity's criteria of equality and need, and believe that market procedures are more fair than political procedures. They are satisfied that they receive what they deserve in the market, but much less satisfied with what they receive in the polity. (p. 386)

That cost-effectiveness, lean structures, and fiscal restraint emerge as key words among administrators, even in social services, is consequently no surprise. But how these sentiments are made operational in welfare activities is an interesting question in social change and an interesting illustration of how two currents blend together—the market forces of post-industrial capitalism and the more socialistic traditions of industrial capitalism. Although hostility to much welfare is now considerable, there is little chance that welfare simply will disappear—evaporate as an interesting experiment gone awry (O'Connor 1973). Health, welfare, education, security—these are considered to be "rights" and are not easily dismissed. As numerous observers have noticed, it may in fact be virtually impossible to reverse the rising tide of entitlement programs.

Several important constituencies mute the conservative attack on welfare. One important source of resistance to cutting public welfare is the recipients themselves. I refer less to the inner-city poor than to the elderly and the broad middle class. The elderly are well-organized. They are less susceptible to political offensives, they are aggressive in their support of cost of living adjustments and entitlement benefits, and they will compose a widening and more powerful base, as demographics shift toward longevity and more active senior citizens. The middle class is protective of its own province: reducing the tax burden through real estate deductions and advancing the case for subsidized health and education.

An additional and interesting constituency in support of welfare is composed of large-scale manufacturing corporations. As a result of widespread prosperity in the 1950s and a willingness to accede to union demands, many corporations today have substantial commitments to pensions and fringe benefits. These corporate interests contend that such commitments cut into their competitiveness with other nations, a claim made convincing by the soaring health costs peculiar to American society. Consequently, manufacturers have a clear stake in expanding government's role in health and welfare and in divesting themselves of past commitments. At the same time, they remain overtly antagonistic to any programs that require future taxes or other corporate obligations.

All of these constituencies—the elderly, the middle class, the manufacturing sector, and other businesses—variously contribute not to the demise of welfare, but to a shift in context: from the public sector to a sector coordinating public-private linkages. The private sector, including certain medical interests, as well as large-scale health providers, are themselves not disinterested parties in this possibility.

Social welfare expenditures, broadly defined, are among the largest expenditures at all levels of government. Privatization breaks the constraints on the use of public resources and puts them to multiple ends: to provide welfare and secure profits. Health and education provide fertile grounds for private-sector development and promise vast sales and riches.

Privatization consequently pledges the fulfillment of two important demands: It offers a way to sustain welfare at reduced cost and in a context rich in opportunities for business initiatives. The assumption behind privatization is simple: That the high costs of welfare reflect the government's hand. And its promise is straightforward: Eliminate the hand, introduce an approximation to the free market, arm practitioners with business knowledge, and costs will decline. Welfare needs consequently can be simply met in a partially regulated but competitive marketplace. Older welfare organizations entrenched in large-scale governmental bureaucracies become history, transitional steps, in this view, in an evolutionary path toward a wide-ranging and extensive market economy. Governmental welfare bureaucracies, as Gary Becker (1992) has argued, face a destiny similar to the failed socialist economies of China and the Soviet Union: Dinosaurs doomed to extinction in an era of free-market enterprise.

THE PRIVATIZATION OF WELFARE: ACROSS THE INSTITUTIONAL DIVIDE

Can the rigors of the competitive market and the more rationalized strategies associated with post-industrial capitalism provide welfare services at a high level of quality and at reduced costs? In previous chapters, I argued that recent developments associated with post-industrial capitalism, including an increase in business knowledge, more flexible organizational structures, and growing managerial and professional expertise, have allowed corporations to generate high sales, and sometimes substantial profits. But whether this experience can translate into the public sector is complicated by the peculiarities of privatization as an uncommon example of social change. In most instances, as previously noted, social change involving emulation is confined within an institutional sector—within the economy, for example (Scott and Meyer 1991). With privatization, however, institutional boundaries are crossed. The new structural grid placed over existing institutional functions signals an important concern as to whether privatization will be able to perform the older functions associated with welfare and preserve the equity associated with citizenship. Before turning to this issue, I must first briefly outline what has been reviewed more extensively elsewhere: the privatization thesis itself, so as to indicate what it is, what it involves, and what precisely is at stake.

The Privatization Position

Privatization is not a simple transfer of welfare to the private sector. Privatization links private development to public goods and also tries to solve some dilemmas of welfare economics. Specifically, the privatization thesis is concerned with market mechanisms. The thesis addresses the issue of market failure and the government's role in the economy. Failure involves "public goods." Public goods spread benefits across society. These benefits are indivisible but they also are indirect. Not all individuals are willing to pay their costs, opting instead to be "free riders" (Olson 1965). Consequently, the market may be unable to sustain an educational system or adequate health care. Much of the recent discussion of nationalized health involves the failure of the market to provide adequate care. Because education and health are important services, governments bypass the market and provide these services directly.

Privatization theorists idealize the free-market economy in criticizing the public sector. In their view, the market's absence creates several problems. In the public sector, prices for welfare are set by fiat rather than by competition or supply and demand. In addition, consumers are locked into the government as the sole provider of certain services. People are unable to shop for low-cost schooling, for social security or income assistance. Consequently, consumer preferences are unknown. In the absence of competition and consumer response, bureaucrats lack motivation to reduce costs and increase efficiency. Cost and price are the primary institutional characteristics privatization theorists consider essential.

To solve the problems of public inefficiency, advocates of privatization recommend options for introducing markets into public welfare. Two mechanisms coordinate this hybrid arrangement crossing public and private domains. One alternative invites competition through periodic bids for government contracts (Poole 1983). Periodic bids allow governments to monitor welfare and guard against opportunism by private providers. Bids also stimulate private initiative and competition. The presumption is that competition will stimulate managerial systems to reduce costs and increase efficiency.

A second mechanism recommended by privatization theorists circumvents the problem of pricing and the public good. Pricing denies equal access to social welfare. On the other hand, free governmental services have undesirable consequences. Free services may be used indiscriminately; consumers have little inducement to avoid costly providers. To solve this problem, advocates of privatization recommend vouchers (Savas 1977a). Vouchers are limited currencies, exchangeable for certain goods or services—housing, food, education. They also are free and consequently equalize access. Because only finite numbers of vouchers are distributed, indiscriminate and unlimited use is restricted. In theory, firms receive vouchers instead of public funding. Costly and inefficient providers will not collect a sufficient number of vouchers to support themselves. Consequently they may fail. Failure is a desirable outcome because, in the view of privatization theorists, government support protects inefficient and costly providers.

These two market forces—from competition and bidding, from vouchers and consumers—serve to reduce costs and to increase flexibility, at least in comparison with the monolithic government welfare bureaucracy. The use of these two forces parallels other more flexible and less bureaucratic processes common to post-industrial capitalism. But these forces have an additional job as well. The job is related to the potential dangers of placing welfare, and the concerns of life and dignity, into a context driven by profit. Opportunism reflects the danger of profit-driven firms compromising quality or equal access to welfare. Competition and vouchers monitor opportunism. Vouchers and competitive bidding empower governments and consumers to oversee private welfare agencies and to select out low quality and high costs. In brief, privatization is seen as an efficient response to the problems of supplying welfare services at a cost consistent with consumer demand. What is offered is a perfect solution to the fiscal difficulties of the welfare state. But there is some question as to whether this ideal-type model works as proposed.

Business and Welfare: Multiple Logics in the Institutional Order

The source of most difficulties in privatization relate to the multiple logics involved in the linkages of the public and private sector— the varying institutional interests of businesses and social services (Friedland and Alford 1991). Social welfare is a mutual support function to distribute and redistribute services and resources so as to sustain or alter the life chances of individuals (Bell 1976; Gilbert and Sprecht 1986; Titmuss 1963). It is a right, a guarantee by the state, that particular needs of the citizenry will be addressed and met (Marshall 1965). Rights imply that all in society will have equal access to basic resources, be it education, health, or other benefits. But in business, there is no intent that equity or equality will be addressed or resolved. The marketplace rewards those who have the most—whether money, knowledge, competitive talent, or guile.

In traditional social theory (Parsons 1951), health, education, and welfare are guided by technical systems of expertise and regulated by nonmarket norms. The norms speak of service in terms of need rather than gain. The understanding legitimating these norms is that they safeguard the public. The literature on the professions underlines the importance of socialization to professional norms, to norms apart from profit-based motives. Sinclair Lewis's (1945) characterization of *Arrowsmith* romantically cast this image of the professional—the selfless, dedicated medical researcher. In comparison, business is about self-interests more than about the collective good. No one, including the advocates of privatization, sees privatization as an issue of corporate benevolence. As one leading advocate of privatization noted, "An ultimate profit is the bottom line. There are no exceptions, for business does nothing unless it can see some benefit for itself or its investors" (Carroll and Easton 1987, p. 20).

Additional complications in privatization result from the variance in tasks across institutions. Consider as an illustration the tasks involved in most welfare activities. Welfare is both more complex and more uncertain than most private-sector products and services. Consequently, the costs incurred in welfare activities are more intractable as well. First, in operational terms, welfare involves the use of applied principles from medicine, health, counseling, and education. Because principles in these fields involve statistical relationships with modest levels of probabilities, their use in welfare policy reflects much uncertainty. Knowledge is simply insufficient to foresee new contingencies. Second, welfare is a service, an interpersonal transaction where professionals do something for their clients or patients. Interpersonal interaction is rarely as straightforward as the rhythms of a machine, but welfare activities suggest additional uncertainty. Thompson (1967) used the term *intensive technology* to describe how clients are used reactively for feedback and insight for further treatment. Client reactions introduce unknowns difficult to foresee. Third, uncertainty is compounded by the frequent inability of clients to articulate their needs—having only vague complaints or unclear desires. Students want to do something significant in an area, but do not know how to proceed. Patients are not feeling well, certain only that they are less robust than in the past. The lack of clarity in clients, and the consequent need for careful diagnosis of problems, are additional sources of uncertainty in welfare situations. These same sources of uncertainty complicate evaluating the success of services—to determine when the case is closed, the problem solved, the cure affected.

Privatization and the Limitations of Managerial Strategies

Privatized welfare introduces market economic norms into the domains formerly governed by welfare professionals and governmental officials. Past writings on privatization suggest that this occurs in several different ways (Kamerman and Kahn 1989; Pack 1987; Starr 1989). First, privatized firms (in comparison to public-sector organizations) make greater use of managers and professionals expert in business administration. Second, and related to this, is the increased use of business criteria in professional judgments. In some instances, as in systems of managed care, professional judgments are formulated according to explicit economic cost-benefit analyses. Also, business staffs are vested with significant authority, although this may vary with the prestige of the profession (Freidson 1984). In this way, the managerial revolution comes to roost in the arena of social welfare.

But the ability of business managers to fulfill their promise in sustaining quality, sustaining equity, and reducing costs—this is more problematic. In some instances, the competitive stance itself generates costs in proliferating expensive technologies useful primarily to attract customers.

In other instances, time-honored procedures for reducing costs are either out of the question or their utility is simply diminished. Consider the following handful of illustrations, all formerly discussed as commonplace practices in strategic management:

1. *Increased Sales.* The expansion of sales is the propellant behind nearly all managerial strategies. Advertising, service, publicity, marketing, and merchandising all are ultimately designed to expand sales. The proposition is simple enough: expanding sales increases revenues and consequently escalates profits, sometimes with lower margins useful for a competitive edge. But the message—buy more, drink more, use more—nobody would recommend that these be considered in privatized welfare.

2. *Customer Marketing.* Many managerial strategies simply conflict with welfare requirements to sustain quality and maintain equity. This is particularly true of strategies based on principles of product differentiation, marketing, and sales. Many strategies cater to specific clients but ignore the needs of others. Some, for example, concentrate on profitable clients. Others vary quality for different levels of consumer income. Still others ignore nonprofitable services or assume a posture of "buyer beware." All are legitimate activities in the market. But they violate the equity norms of social welfare.

3. *Aggressive Growth.* In his work on competitive strategies, Porter (1988) recommends procedures for aggressive growth, involving strategic losses in particular areas if they increase market share and undermine the viability of the competition. The understanding is that later gains, under more monopolistic circumstances, might compensate for temporary losses. But although a competitive edge might be the goal for the privatized welfare firm, the ultimate goal could not possibly be total victory—vanquishing the opposition to emerge as the sole provider in an area. This outcome would only replicate the very problem privatized welfare tries to confront: monopoly control over social services.

4. *Costing Strategies.* Many innovations in business involve attempts to costs all activities, from the most incidental to the most important, so as to evaluate their worth. But welfare activities are difficult to cost in light of their uncertain turns and complex structure.

Costs are not easily allocated to identifiable categories in a clear and standardized manner. More to the point, however, is the absence of a metric for the worth and benefit of intangibles—life, health, education—that is easily translated into dollars and cents. Is backup or duplication a vital ingredient during a complex operation or merely slack to be eliminated?

These constraints suggest difficulty in fulfilling the double-barreled promise of privatization: that costs will be lowered and equal access to quality services sustained. Although markets can and do confront the twin issues of equity and efficiency (Okun 1975), they may not easily and simply be able to optimize both equity and efficiency and at the same time sustain quality. I am not suggesting that welfare constraints on cost reduction render managerial strategies useless. Many procedures, for example, are neither complex nor uncertain. Nonetheless, markets will best be able to use managerial strategies to reduce costs when free to pursue a variety of alternatives—to advertise, to market, to sell, and to track complex costs.

In brief, the anticipation of the market's ability to deliver welfare fairly and equitably may be unrealistic. In fact the privatization view seems riddled with assumptions that may be more guided by ideological conviction and commitment to the market than to a realistic understanding of what welfare is about. Quite simply, privatization may do much to increase price and diminish quality. The constraints on managerial strategies to affect costs put pressure on other alternatives for meeting competition by restricting access, decreasing quality, or diminishing costs through increased sales and use. If welfare provisions deteriorate, there is little question of the result: The very rich, those with unlimited funds, simply will go around the existing system and use what is available in the unregulated private sector. Those without resources, however, will have to make do with whatever exists. And if what exists is both restrictive and shoddy in character and quality, then the burdens of such treatment fall on the poor.

COSTS IN PRIVATIZATION: FACTS AND MYTHS

The Routine Costs of Public Goods

Public-private alliances are likely the wave of the future. It is consequently important to outline precisely what private development can contribute to the public sector. One possibility, following Meyer and Rowan (1977), is that privatization elaborates "a rationalized institutional myth"—with public functions assuming the cloak of rational business and gaining resources and legitimacy in turn. In this view, technical efficiencies are the mythical component of an organizational facade, of the face of private enterprise. On the other hand, privatization may actually contribute to technical efficiency, reducing costs, and increasing efficiency and productivity, as privatization theorists suggest. My argument is that both outcomes occur, each contingent on the actual substance and content of the privatized activity.

In the standard defense of privatization, public-private cost comparisons on standardized goods and services show superior performance in the private sector. Privatization advocates, for example, cite a long list of privatized, routine services where costs have been reduced. Studies indicate lower costs associated with privatization in refuse collection, claims processing, ship repair, utilities, airline services, solid waste, school busing, fire protection, prisons, mail delivery, and urban transportation (Bennett and Johnson 1980; Carroll and Easton 1987; Morlock and Vitton 1985; Poole and Fixler 1987; Savas 1977b). These studies, in the view of privatization advocates, confirm the cost-consciousness and "bottom line" mentality of the private sector.

The comparison of public-private costs suggests that superiority in public-sector performance can be extended to welfare—to activities more uncertain and more complex, requiring more professional presence and input. But the merits of this suggestion are not clear. In Bennett and Johnson's (1980) widely cited review of private-sector superiority, for example, social welfare services are sparsely represented. Bennett and Johnson (1980) do suggest that economies have been achieved in medical care. But the evidence in these studies is not convincing. In the three studies cited, these authors compare the public and nonprofit sector rather than the private sector as such. In one of the three studies, prices are actually higher (although quality is lower). Most important, Bennett and Johnson ignore that the private sector's economies in welfare usually reflect savings on intermediate products (Pack 1987). Studies report economies in regard to drugs, eye glasses, office equipment, and other purchases of routine goods with easily defined qualities (General Accounting Office 1986; Lawrence et al. 1981). But the overall influence of such purchases on welfare costs is not likely to be significant, particularly if the welfare area in question has substantial commitments to professional wages and technology.

This research consequently suggests that privatization proposals are likely correct in instances where expenditures involve many standardized products and simple, more routinized activities. In other instances, closer to welfare services, privatization may be more of a high-risk activity. This is consistent with research indicating, contrary to common public perceptions, that public sectors are not necessarily bloated, wasteful, and inefficient nor are they likely to be more costly to administer than the private sector; sometimes the reverse is the case (Downs and Larkey 1986; General Accounting Office 1986; Hannaway 1987; Prinsky 1978). At least with respect to complex welfare functions, it is conceivable that privatization is a rationalized myth, and that lower costs in privatized welfare only can be accomplished by scaling back quality and limiting access to scarce resources.

Privatization and Costs in the Production of Welfare

The privatization argument rates the private sector as more capable than the public sector in reducing costs. But my argument is that the high costs of welfare reflect its uncertainty and complexity and, further, that cost-cutting procedures are difficult to implement. From this view, high costs in welfare reflect less the inefficiencies of government or the failure to be competitive than the expenses associated with professional personnel; the intensive use of labor to track uncertain and complex problems; the difficulty and extensive use of diagnosis for problem evaluation; costly technology at the edge of innovation; and sensitivity to the growth in new problems (such as AIDS) and greater recognition of old problems (such as Alzheimer's disease) that are ill understood.

Higher and legitimate welfare costs have not kept privatization theorists from recommending market alternatives. These recommendations, however, ignore the dozens of studies on medical care indicating that public institutions are nearly always lower priced than for-profit institutions. Many of these studies concentrate on comparisons between profit and nonprofit institutions (rather than on public and private institutions). But they investigate a key point in privatization writings: the role of profit and competition in reducing costs and increasing efficiencies. In reviewing the research in this area, a study sponsored by the National Academy of Science concluded the following:

> Studies of hospitals provide no evidence to support the common belief that investor-owned organizations are less costly or more efficient than are not-for-profit organizations. . . . [Available] studies that have controlled for many confounding factors including distinguishing investor-owned from independent proprietary hospitals show the opposite to be true. (Gray 1986, p. 1525)

Although limited to a specific setting, these findings challenge the profit motive and competition of the private sector as important in increasing efficiency and reducing client costs. This is no accident or surprise. Profit-based firms are supposed to reduce costs but, as Eli Ginzberg (1990) suggests, they may (counterintuitively) increase them: by adding costs for profits, advertising, and marketing, by duplicating technology, and by increasing capacity for purposes of competition. Most of all, privatized welfare firms encourage publics to use more than they need. If these effects are widespread, managerial skills may be more aligned with increasing profits than with reducing costs.

If costs are high in private activities, and if managerial strategies are inadequate for reducing the costs associated with complex and uncertain tasks, then how can economies be achieved by private firms? In managing costs, the private sector uses the full array of schemes available. Welfare costs are analyzed and expenditures evaluated against benefits. Several outcomes are possible, related to limiting either costs or access. One alternative reexamines costs, particularly labor, and strives to attain a more inexpensive mix. Research suggests that among privatized firms in welfare, the most likely alternative for decreasing costs cuts labor costs directly: by reducing professional staff, by substituting paraprofessionals for professionals, or by simply reducing staff pay (Bendick 1989; Schlesinger et al. 1986). The issue of paraprofessionals and their impact on quality has generated much debate and discussion (Light 1986). But the complexity and uncertainty of tasks traditionally involved in welfare suggest rather narrow limits on substituting for professional skills and expertise (see Stinchcombe 1990).

Privatization theorists assume that competitive bidding is an effective way to lower costs. But several studies indicate problems in competitive bidding; they also suggest multiple difficulties in lowering costs. If cost cutting is constrained both by the complexity of the task and welfare demands for equity, then bidding is unlikely to be successful. The most extensive research on competitive bidding for welfare involved contracts invited by the Massachusetts Department of Health (Schlesinger et al. 1986). Two thirds of all bids submitted were from a single vendor. Only 15% were from more than two vendors, leading the state auditor to comment on the absence of qualified providers for competition. The private firms selected reduced costs by cutting salaries for all workers, professionals included. The cuts, however, resulted in extraordinary turnover, averaging 40% across units. The authors report numerous complaints about quality and extreme discontinuity in the treatment of chronic illness. Also, although agency costs were lower, the overhead incurred by the state to pay for bidding and monitoring procedures raised total governmental expenses to a level higher than those prior to the subcontracting procedure.

The Office of Economic Opportunity's experiment in education replicated Massachusetts' disastrous experience with competitive bidding. The call for bidding generated 31 responses, but only 12 qualified contractors. Of these, the proportion of quality professionals was generally low, as indicated by the extensive use of paraprofessionals, ranging from 40% to 100% of the staff involved. Quality was uneven. Test scores among students in the experiment rose modestly in some academic subjects but fell in others. The firms involved reported they lost money. No contracts were renewed, and the relationships were frequently terminated with ill feeling and acrimony (Gramlich and Koshel 1975). Other studies underscore the absence of qualified providers. Straussman's (1981) work in Rochester, New York, reports multiple providers only in homemaker services but not among more skilled welfare activities. A study of social service contracting in Massachusetts likewise indicated limited providers in social services (Gurin and Friedman 1981). These studies are inconsistent with the privatization position that competition clearly produces quality providers.

Constraining access or charges is another alternative for limiting the costs in welfare. One option imposes rigid diagnoses and cost ceilings on services, hence restricting additional but ancillary benefits and costs. In health care, for example, these alternatives are widely available with computer software or from utilization management firms that impose diagnoses and recommended procedures in some form of managed care. Or access may be limited and waiting periods enacted, thus reducing costs for additional staff, facilities, or technology. But these procedures are not wholly satisfactory. Cost containment in medical care, for example, has a poor record in handling unforeseen contingencies that are complex and uncertain. Lindberg and his colleagues (1989) review extensive research indicating high incidences of mortality among elderly patients in areas where rigid cost containment procedures have been imposed. This outcome is not surprising. There is considerable variability within diagnostic categories; cost containment, however, imposes more uniform treatment.

These conclusions on cost containment are in line with a more general position that if private welfare firms cut costs (or prices), quality declines; if quality is sustained, then prices are high and not appreciably different than those incurred by public firms. In brief, the constraints on cost reduction in welfare make it likely that quality and costs will be inversely related. For example, most of the hospital studies examined in Gray's (1986) previously cited review indicated comparable quality among profits and nonprofits but higher charges in the for-profit firms. Private firms under contract to county hospitals in California showed neither reductions in costs nor increases in quality (Shonick and Roemer 1982). On the other hand, private firms under contract to 100 local school districts produced modest improvements in test scores but substantial losses of money (Bendick 1984). Similar findings indicating a reverse relationship between quality and costs also have been reported for nursing home facilities and privatized child care centers (Hawes and Phillips 1986; Kamerman and Kahn 1989). These findings uniformly contradict the private firm's alleged superiority in reducing costs without altering effectiveness. If costs are increased, quality is sustained; if costs are reduced, quality suffers. In the arena of welfare, managerial initiatives to limit costs have clear limitations.

EVALUATING PRIVATIZATION:
PROBLEMS AND DIFFICULTIES

There is reason to believe that a rationalized myth indeed surrounds privatization: that costs do not decline and that competition significantly detracts from quality or access. Privatization advocates discuss two options to guard against dysfunctions of this kind. One option involves bidding and governmental surveillance, where governmental agencies periodically invite new bids, providing occasion to review past performance in quality and costs. Another option relies on consumer preferences, with consumers having the aptitude and good sense to avoid providers with deteriorating quality or highly restrictive access. These two mechanisms are designed to minimize systemic dysfunctions.

Institutional theorists, however, conceptualize systemic dysfunctions from another vantage point. Meyer and Rowan (1977), for example, discuss organizational change in terms of the prestige and legitimation it brings about. Because change, in their view, is frequently grounded in legitimation rather than in gains in technical efficiency, technical operating systems are decoupled from everyday affairs. In other words, no one examines how or whether the system is working—thus engaging in what Talcott Parsons (1951) called pattern evasion.

In the privatization of welfare, however, other factors may sustain technical inefficiencies, different from Meyer and Rowan's decoupling process and in contrast to the safeguards privatization advocates suggest. The differences relate to the complexity and uncertainty of welfare. Because much welfare activity is run by professionals and understood in highly technical terms, the activities involved are frequently difficult for lay people to evaluate and for governments to monitor easily. As a consequence, dysfunctional activity may go unnoticed, not because the system is decoupled, in Meyer and Rowan's terms, but because it is difficult to rationalize and structured so that few are capable of evaluating indications of dysfunction. Welfare managers then might cut quality or access, but without an effective check on their behavior.

Government Surveillance

The most caustic critique of privatization implicates private agencies for bypassing social obligations and following easy routes to profits. One example of this type of opportunism is referred to as "skimming" or "creaming" clients. Studies on hospitals, for example, allege that administrators select sites located in suburban settings populated by affluent individuals with few health problems that are easy to treat (Demone and Gibleman 1987). Kamerman and Kahn's (1989) study of the privatization of child care notes that:

> Most private, for-profit providers—the large commercial chains, for example—will not locate their services in low-income neighborhoods. Time and again senior executives of these firms explain their marketing strategies by stressing careful selection of sites. A major highway, a location between a middle-class residential area and a commercial area, a community with high female labor-force participation rates, and husband-and-wife families with two earners and incomes more than 50 percent above median family income—these are what they seek. (pp. 248-49)

The less problematic the client or patient, the higher the client income, the easier and less costly they are to treat—and the greater the profits.

Privatization advocates are aware of skimming. They also are aware that skimming is in direct violation of equity requirements associated with social welfare. To guard against its occurrence, they feel that private welfare agencies should be evaluated periodically on their costs, their quality, and the scope of their coverage. The bidding process explicitly is designed to monitor quality, equity, and opportunism. On periodic occasions, businesses resubmit bids for governmental contracts. Data on quality and cost performance are reviewed. Contracts presumably are awarded to firms with the lowest costs and the best track records in performance.

But periodic reviews of privatized welfare may be more problematic than they appear. Public institutions draw on richer resources and greater expertise than ordinary individuals. But the difficulty in drawing on this expertise relates back to my initial premise: Welfare tasks are complex, uncertain, difficult to rationalize, and not easy to evaluate in terms of costs. For this reason, government contracts for welfare are problematic to write and demanding to monitor (Sappington and Stiglitz 1987; Williamson 1981). As one expert on the economics of the public sector has noted:

> It may be difficult to specify precisely the characteristics of the product or service that is to be provided and to ensure that the desired "quality" is maintained. While it is possible to contract for the delivery of a specific tank or plane . . . could local governments write a contract with private schools to produce the kind of education the community wishes? Would it have to supervise what is done so closely that it might as well

take direct control to ensure that the desired "quality" is maintained?
(Stiglitz 1988, pp. 192-93)

In Williamson's (1981) transaction theory, the difficulty in tracking
uncertainty is one of the factors contributing to the internalization of
organizational activities. Privatization, however, moves in the opposite direction: externalizing welfare functions from the government
and shifting course from hierarchy to market.

The methodology for evaluation research is well-established (Patton
1982). But there is considerable consensus that governments are
ill-equipped to evaluate programs to capture the elusive characteristics of quality care and equal access. Perrow (1970) notes that
most public-sector evaluations devolve into head counts: the number
of students graduated, prisoners served, or hospital beds filled. In a
study of social welfare agencies, Gurin (1989) points out that governments limited monitoring to fiscal issues, and where they attempted
to go beyond this, they were quickly overwhelmed. Weisbrod and
Schlesinger (1986) similarly note that most governmental agencies
confine themselves to criteria easily evaluated, such as sanitation or
staff and patient ratios, rather than the complexities of estimating
competence or humanity. Furthermore, governments are fiscally
strapped with difficulty in sustaining their day-to-day operations.
To monitor social programs effectively is probably beyond the capacity of most governmental agencies. Regulation is an easily understood concept, but its implementation is not straightforward.

Consumer Choice and Citizenship Rights

If governments experience difficulty monitoring the performance
of privatized welfare firms, could individuals possibly monitor welfare providers more effectively? The answer should be apparent. But
this has not deterred privatization advocates from placing the burden of access on individuals. By approximating a free market, individuals are, according to the privatization argument, themselves
responsible for choice. Individuals consequently should choose the
schools they attend, the health centers they frequent, and the care
provided for their children. Free choice is important in privatization
theory. Free choice by consumers monitors opportunism and also
ensures the selection of worthwhile economies. Great faith is placed
in the wisdom of the free market. Although free choice is a laudable

aim, a nagging question is whether consumers behave as privatization theorists maintain.

A major difficulty with privatization relates to the high level of rationality assumed to exist among consumers. The assumption of rationality is among the most widely criticized characteristics of classical economics (Arrow 1974; Cyret and March 1963; Simon 1957). The complexities in welfare pose problems in addition to those implied in the critique of rational man. These problems suggest that although few tasks are simple, evaluating a therapist, physician, or school is even less straightforward.

The problems of rationality in selecting welfare services stem from the complexity and uncertainty of the task. The problems reflect the skewed knowledge distribution between client and professional. Clients, for example, may be unsure what if anything is wrong or what has to be done. The criteria for adequate education in school or cure in medicine or psychotherapy are more difficult to specify than for most everyday goods and services. Comparisons among competitors are easiest in repetitive tasks with clearly observable outcomes. But clear outcomes are infrequent and most welfare services not repetitive. In numerous welfare services, the outcome is long term and may be difficult to evaluate in shorter time intervals. In fact, knowledge about outcomes is frequently so unclear that clients abdicate authority to professionals regarding how and whether to proceed with treatment or service.

In the extreme, uncertain and complex problems lack any clear solution. But this has not deterred privatization theorists from recommending private-sector alternatives. Consider the use of vouchers for public school selection. Vouchers are consistent with privatization goals to optimize free choice and competition among schools. Viable competition, however, is predicated on discernible school effects on student development. But after decades of research, the consensus is that contextual school effects are small, potentially nonexistent, and extraordinarily difficult to spot and interpret correctly (Jencks 1985). How then can parents select schools judiciously?

Similar problems of comparison and choice plague other welfare activities, as in evaluating the varying success rates among hospitals for medical procedures. The Health Care Financing Administration publishes mortality rates for about 6,000 hospitals in this country. Reports on local hospitals regularly show up in local newspapers. But what do such statistics reflect? Are they valid barometers to facilitate selecting hospitals? As indicated by much research, medical failure is difficult to interpret, reflecting patient mix and other factors related to organizational structure (Flood and Scott 1987). Complex causal modeling may be required. But this is not easily done by professionals, let alone ordinary consumers.

Problems of rationality are complicated further by the class backgrounds of welfare recipients. Welfare consumers are frequently not middle-class individuals armed with the time, energy, motivation, and information necessary to monitor quality and costs. Many are from the lower strata. The potential relation between evaluation and social class also complicates choice. If class influenced rationality and choice, the distribution of welfare might approximate the unequal distribution of private goods. The issue is important because many welfare recipients experience a wide range of social problems: unemployment, illiteracy, illness, and poverty (Prottas 1979). These individuals also are extremely vulnerable to the possible opportunism in the private sector.

The lower strata's difficulty in coping with large-scale institutions and welfare agencies has been documented extensively (Hasenfeld 1985; Sjoberg and Brymer 1966). Evidence suggests that middle-class individuals benefit from opportunities for free choice in selecting welfare options. A recent Carnegie report, for example, indicates that if schools differ widely in quality, middle-class individuals will flock to better schools, whereas those lower in status will remain in distinctly poorer educational facilities (*New York Times* 1992d). Kamerman and Kahn's (1989) analysis of the privatization of child care similarly shows that lower strata families are less likely to use available tax credits, thus increasing disparities in care quality in comparison to the middle class.

In brief, complex welfare services make rationality difficult to exercise, particularly for the disadvantaged. This is as true, of course, in the public as in the private sector. But in the privatized sector rationality plays a pivotal role. According to privatization theorists, the burden on the consumer is to monitor services so that high-quality, low-cost providers are selected. The failure to do this effectively means that inefficient and opportunistic providers may survive and the advantage of the private sector lost.

CONCLUSION

Post-industrial capitalism diminishes and reverses the historic trend toward greater equality. Under post-industrial capitalism, the influence of the market increases along several dimensions. Markets expand in scope. They take on international dimensions by breaking down national barriers and furthering competition. Markets change. Managerial techniques and producer services add new routes to profits, supplementing and enriching the traditional production and distribution of goods and services. Markets expand into new institutions and new domains such as welfare, which were previously organized according to need and service rather than price and profit.

The spread of the market to the public sector reflects the movement of capitalism across the institutional order. This movement is most dramatically reflected in the privatization of welfare. Privatization is a monumental experiment. At stake is whether the marketplace can improve all forms of social organization. Its potential is clear: to decrease the costs of welfare in a format that promises quality and efficiency. The format couples the competition of the marketplace with the expertise, the managerial strategies, and know-how of the business community. Privatization attempts to rationalize social services, to put it on the same footing, with the same techniques and skills that exist in private enterprise. Privatization guarantees that welfare will be competitive. But whether managerial strategies can be used to advantage is more questionable. These strategies, honed in the private sector to reduce costs and increase efficiency, may be constrained by the characteristics of welfare itself: in the complexity and uncertainty of the task and in the normative commitment to quality and equity.

I suggest limits to the strategies and techniques associated with management under post-industrial capitalism. These techniques have been unusually successful in the private sector, both domestically and internationally, in increasing sales and profits. But they are not easily transposed into the public domain of health, education, and welfare. Where used they frequently drive up costs, decrease quality, or alter equity in access. Research on this issue is admittedly ambiguous, with sophisticated studies lacking. Nonetheless, the numerous assumptions about the market and the anticipation of benefits in private-sector delivery are not widely supported. In all sectors, private enterprise increases competition and inequality.

I must add that my critique of privatization is no defense of a status quo in welfare. Reform is a priority. Welfare is excessively bureaucratic. Possibly more freedom of choice is necessary to break down the monopoly of agencies or schools on clients, so as to effect a better match in interests and concerns. Possibly too, the cumbersome bureaucracy should be decentralized to diminish redundancy and allow localized response and innovation. But transferring ownership is not equivalent to making units smaller, more autonomous, or available to clients in wider areas of residence, as privatization theorists sometimes assume. The concern here is not with the need for reform but with the specific agent of change.

Postscript

Inequality Without Class Conflict

Ideology, according to Daniel Bell, is at an end. The utopian ideas that fueled the beliefs and commitments of a former age are now exhausted. Writing in the early 1960s, Bell (1962) commented that

> the politics of the decade, which is at the root of the recent social changes, derives from wholly different impulses than those of twenty years ago. The politics of the 1930s was almost entirely domestic in its focus, and the social cleavages of that period were internal, almost class cleavages, in socio-economic terms. Little of this has meaning today, nor are the alignments of twenty years ago the same as those of the last decade. Politics today is not a reflex of any internal class divisions. (p. 14)

What is of issue today, according to Bell, are status aspirations. These aspirations rewrite the political agenda. They diminish the utility of a conventional class analysis of American society.

Bell was right—but only up to a point. America, after all, was (and continues to be) highly stratified. Economic disparities remain. Poverty and inequality in recent years have increased. But Bell was correct in his estimate that by the end of World War II, overt class

157

schisms were a thing of the past. The Marxist vision that framed class analysis no longer applied clearly and simply to the American case.

Residues of class-related factors lingered on. Writing in 1960, Seymour Martin Lipset spoke of the "democratization of the class struggle"—the implication being that class conflict shifted out of the factory and into the ballot box. Norman Birnbaum (1969, p. 5) discussed reconsidering class in terms of labor unions and labor strikes as the "more profane forms of antagonism" that form the "stuff of modern class conflict." But even voting and unions began to erode just a decade or two later. By the 1980s, class voting was barely discernible. Union membership diminished to its lowest point in more than 50 years. Labor militance was virtually nonexistent.

Three factors contributed to declining class schisms, in accentuating a concern with equity and in restraining the divide between the rich and the poor (Nelson 1981):

1. A highly productive economy with monopoly firms dominating the market and controlling profits
2. A system of labor relations stimulating rising wages
3. A welfare structure effectively redistributing wealth and income

The aftermath of World War II, particularly the intact infrastructure in the United States, further diminished class schisms. In comparison to international competitors, particularly Germany and Japan, America was sovereign. With sovereignty, economic development was joined to social development. The goals of labor and capital appeared to coincide, providing an illusion of victory for both capitalism and socialism.

The demise of class conflict, from the perspective of classical social theory, is symptomatic of diminishing social problems (Coser 1956). In Marxist thought, conflict marches in tandem with inequality. But the 1980s and 1990s unravelled a new thread to this perspective: the collapse of working-class ideology, a sharp decline in class conflict—but all in a climate of growing economic inequities.

From the perspective of traditional theory, recent developments do not make good sociological sense. They suggest the simple conclusion that these perspectives are faulty. In my view, traditional theory fails to account for a new order, one with heightened importance given to the market economy, with increased pressure on wages, and with more influential and extensive control of business over politics. Out of this new order, business leaders fashioned a more conservative consensus, indicating that economic competition is a key aim of Americans everywhere. On this, there is now little public dissent.

The theory of post-industrial capitalism addresses these recent developments. As with other arguments, post-industrial capitalism considers the most recent and influential trends across the institutional spectrum: in an increased ability to communicate rapidly and transport cheaply, in growing affluence, and in changing gender roles and household composition. But the perspective looks as well to the ability of business to capitalize on these events. Owing to increased use of strategic management, to the growing knowledge base of business, and to greater organizational flexibility, business has been more able than in the past to increase its political domination and to intensify and widen economically competitive fields. Inequality in the absence of conflict is the result—suggesting little political opposition in the near future to increased inequality or to the growing importance and influence of the business community.

It is unclear how long these arrangements will persist or what a more distant future holds. But this much is clear: Recent events have taken their toll. Public opinion polls show increased distrust of Americans toward government and politicians. Advocates of business legitimate ideas that businesses and the market are the best and most efficient form of social organization. The staggering growth of business services, growth greater than any other service activity, provides the resources, the alternatives, and the rationale for the spread of the market as a model of organization. Producer services are the new experts. Professionals and managers schooled in business administration are the applied arm of free-market economics, providing expertise, advice, and direction in the spread of the marketplace.

The consequence of all of this is the market triumphant. Markets are everywhere, and everywhere they are considered the most efficient form of social organization across the institutional order. The ascendence of the market, its importance for an ever wider array of decisions, and its movement across institutions—all of this represents uncharted waters. These developments are critical. They do not bode well for equity. Markets are not about justice. They are about profits. There is nothing wrong with the pursuit of profits, if market excesses can be handled according to human need and dignity. Some provisions for need and dignity were present in the era of industrial capitalism. In the era of post-industrial capitalism, these provisions diminish.

References

Aaronson, Susan. 1992. "Serving America's Business? Graduate Business Schools and American Business, 1945-60." *Business History* 34:160-82.

Aglietta, Michel. 1979. *A Theory of Capitalist Regulation: The U.S. Experience*. London: NLB.

Akard, Patrick J. 1992. "Corporate Mobilization and Political Power: The Transformation of U.S. Economic Policy in the 1970s." *American Sociological Review* 57:597-615.

Ansoff, H. Igor. 1965. *Corporate Strategy*. New York: McGraw-Hill.

Arrow, Kenneth. 1974. *The Limits of Organization*. New York: Norton.

Astin, Alexander, Kenneth Green, and William S. Korn. 1987. *The American Freshman: Twenty-Year Trends*. Los Angeles: Cooperative Institutional Research Program, University of California, Los Angeles.

Baden-Fuller, Charles and John Stoppard. 1991. "Globalization Frustrated." *Strategic Management Journal* 12:493-507.

Bairoch, Paul. 1982. "International Industrialization Levels from 1750 to 1980." *Journal of European Economic History* 11:269-310.

Baker, Wayne. 1990. "Market Networks and Corporate Behavior." *American Journal of Sociology* 96:589-625.

Baron, James, Frank Dobbin, and P. Devereaux Jennings. 1986. "War and Peace: The Evolution of Modern Personnel Administration in U.S. Industry." *American Journal of Sociology* 92:350-83.

Bass, Frank M., Phillipe Cattin, and Dick Witinick. 1978. "Firm Effects and Industry Effects in the Analyses of Market Structure and Profitability." *Journal of Marketing Research* 15:3-10.

Baumol, William J., Sue Anne Batey Blackman, and Edward N. Wolff. 1989. *Productivity and American Leadership*. Cambridge: MIT Press.

Baysinger, Barry and Richard Woodman. 1982. "Public Affairs and Government Relations in American Corporations." *Strategic Management Journal* 3:27-42.

Bechofer, Frank, Brian Elliott, and Monica Rushford. 1971. "The Market Situation of Small Shopkeepers." *Scottish Journal of Political Economy* 18:161-80.

Becker, Brian. 1988. "Concession Bargaining: The Meaning of Union Gains." *Academy of Management Journal* 31:377-87.

Becker, Gary S. 1992. "Surprises in a World According to Adam Smith." *Business Week*, August 17, p. 18.

Bednarzik, Robert W. 1993. "An Analysis of U.S. Industries Sensitive to Foreign Trade, 1982-87." *Monthly Labor Review* 116:15-31.

Beenstock, Michael. 1984. *The World Economy in Transition*. London: George Allen and Unwin.

Behrman, Jack N. and Richard I. Levin. 1984. "Are Business Schools Doing Their Job?" *Harvard Business Review* 62:140-47.

Bell, Daniel. 1962. *The End of Ideology: On the Exhaustion of Political Ideas in the Fifties*. New York: Collier Books.

Bell, Daniel. 1973. *The Coming of Post-Industrial Society*. New York: Basic Books.

Bell, Daniel. 1976. *The Cultural Contradictions of Capitalism*. New York: Basic Books.

Bendick, Mark. 1984. "Privatization of Public Services: Recent Experience." Pp. 153-71 in *Public-Private Partnership: New Opportunities for Meeting Social Needs*, edited by Harvey Brooks, Lance Liebman, and Corrine Schelling. Cambridge, MA: Ballinger.

Bendick, Mark. 1989. "Privatizing Delivery of Service." Pp. 98-120 in *Privatization and the Welfare State*, edited by Sheila Kamerman and Alfred Kahn. Princeton, NJ: Princeton University Press.

Bennett, James T. and Manuel H. Johnson. 1980. "Tax Reduction Without Sacrifice." *Public Finance Quarterly* 8:363-96.

Bentham, Jeremy. [1789] 1948. *An Introduction to the Principles of Morals and Legislation*. New York: Hafner.

Berle, Adolf A. and Gardiner Means. 1932. *The Modern Corporation and Private Property*. New York: Commerce Clearing House.

Berlin, Isaiah. 1991. *The Crooked Timber of Humanity*. New York: Random House.

Birnbaum, Norman. 1969. *The Crisis of Industrial Society*. New York: Oxford University Press.

Blank, Rebecca. 1991. "Why Were Policy Rates So High in the 1980s?" Working Paper No. 3878, National Bureau of Economic Research, Cambridge, MA.

Blau, Peter M. 1963. *The Dynamics of Bureaucracy*. Chicago: University of Chicago Press.

Blau, Peter M., Wolfe Heydebrand, and Robert Stauffer. 1966. "The Structure of Small Bureaucracies." *American Sociological Review* 31:179-91.

Block, Fred. 1977. *The Origins of International Economic Disorder: A Study of International Monetary Policy from World War II to the Present*. Berkeley: University of California Press.

Bluestone, Barry and Bennett Harrison. 1982. *The Deindustrialization of America*. New York: Basic Books.

Blum, Debra E. 1991. "Business Schools Rush to Revise Curricula in Response to Critics and Competition." *Chronicle of Higher Education* 38:23, 28-29.

Blumenthal, Sidney. 1986. *The Rise of the Counter-Establishment: From Conservative Ideology to Political Power*. New York: Times Books.

Bound, John and George Johnson. 1992. "Changes in the Structure of Wages in the 1980s: An Evaluation of Alternative Explanations." *American Economic Review* 82:371-92.

Boyer, Robert. 1988. *The Search for Labor Market Flexibility*. Oxford: Clarendon Press.

Bradach, Jeffrey and Robert Eccles. 1989. "Price, Authority, and Trust: From Ideal Types to Plural Forms." *Annual Review of Sociology* 15:97-118.

Braverman, Harry. 1975. *Labor and Monopoly Capital*. New York: Monthly Review Press.

Brickley, James and Frederick H. Dark. 1987. "The Choice of Organizational Form: The Case of Franchising." *Journal of Financial Economics* 18:401-20.

Browning, Harley L. and Joachim Singelmann. 1978. "The Transformation of the U.S. Labor Force: The Interaction of Industry and Occupation." *Politics and Society* 8:481-509.

Browning, Harley L. and Joachim Singelmann. 1980. "Industrial Transformation and Occupational Change in the U.S., 1960-1970." *Social Forces* 59:246-64.

Bryant, Keith and Henry Dethloff. 1983. *A History of American Business*. Englewood Cliffs, NJ: Prentice Hall.

Burawoy, Michael. 1979. *Manufacturing Consent: Changes in the Labor Process Under Monopoly Capitalism*. Chicago: University of Chicago Press.

Bureau of National Affairs. 1985. *Labor Relations Consultants: Issues, Trends, and Controversies*. Washington, DC: Bureau of National Affairs.

Burnham, James. 1941. *The Managerial Revolution*. New York: John Day.

Business Week. 1981. "The New Industrial Relations." May 11, pp. 85-98.

Business Week. 1986. "The Hollow Corporation." March 3, pp. 57-59.

Business Week. 1990. "Dispelling the Myths That Are Holding America Back." December 17, pp. 66-70.

Business Week. 1992a. "The Days of Ozzie and Harriet Are Gone for Good." February 10, p. 16.

Business Week. 1992b. "The Global Economy: Who Get's Hurt?" August 10, pp. 48-53.

Business Week. 1992c. "Who'll Get the Lion's Share of Wealth in the '90s?" June 8, pp. 86-88.

Buzzell, Robert and Bradley Gale. 1987. *The PIMS Principle*. New York: Free Press.

Cappelli, Peter and John Chalykoff. 1986. "The Effects of Management Industrial Relations Strategy: Results of a Recent Survey." Pp. 171-78 in *Proceedings of the Thirty-Eighth Annual Meeting of the Industrial Relations Research Association*. Madison: Industrial Relations Research Association, University of Wisconsin.

Carney, Mick and Eric Gedajlovic. 1991. "Vertical Integration in Franchise Systems: Agency Theory and Resource Explanations." *Strategic Management Journal* 12:607-29.

Carroll, Barry J. and Thomas Easton. 1987. "Motivating the Public Sector: What Role for Public Policy?" Pp. 20-49 in *Private Means, Public Ends*, edited by Barry J. Carroll, Ralph Conant, and Thomas Easton. Westport, CT: Praeger.

Castells, Manuel. 1976. "The Service Economy and Postindustrial Society: A Sociological Critique." *International Journal of Health Services* 6:594-607.

Cavanaugh, Thomas. 1981. "Changes in American Voter Turnout, 1964-76." *Political Science Quarterly* 96:53-65.

Chaison, Gary and Dileep Dhavale. 1980. "A Note on the Severity of the Decline in Union Organizing Activity." *International Labor Relations Review* 43:366-73.

Chandler, Alfred. 1977. *The Visible Hand: The Managerial Revolution in American Business*. Cambridge, MA: Belknap Press.

Chandler, Alfred. 1990. *Scale and Scope: The Dynamics of Industrial Capitalism*. Cambridge, MA: Belknap Press.

Chase-Dunn, Christopher. 1987. "Cycles, Trends, or Transformation? The World System Since 1948." Pp. 57-83 in *America's Changing Role in the World System*, edited by Terry Boswell and Albert Bergeson. London: Longmans.

Chase-Dunn, Christopher. 1990. *Global Formation*. Cambridge: Basil Blackwell.

Child, J. 1987. "Information Technology, Organization, and Response to Strategic Challenges." *California Management Review* 30:33-50.

Christopherson, Susan and Michael Storper. 1989. "The Effects of Flexible Specialization on Industrial Politics and the Labor Market: The Motion Picture Industry." *International Labor Relations Review* 42:331-47.

Clawson, Dan. 1980. *Bureaucracy and the Labor Process: The Transformation of Industry.* New York: Monthly Review Press.

Clawson, Dan and Mary Ann Clawson. 1985. "Reagan or Business? Foundations of the New Conservatism." Pp. 201-44 in *The Power Structure of American Business,* edited by Beth Mintz and Michael Schwartz. Chicago: University of Chicago Press.

Cohen, Robert. 1981. "The New Institutional Division of Labor, Multinational Corporations, and Urban Hierarchy." Pp. 287-315 in *Urbanization and Urban Planning in Capitalist Society,* edited by Michael Dear and Allen Scott. London: Metheun.

Committee on Small Business. 1991. *Franchising in Hard Times* (Serial no. 102-10). Washington, DC: Government Printing Office.

Cooper, Mark and Lawrence Soley. 1990. "All the Right Sources." *Mother Jones* 14:20-27.

Cornfield, Daniel. 1986. "Declining Union Membership in the Post-World War II Era." *American Journal of Sociology* 91:1112-53.

Coser, Lewis. 1956. *The Functions of Social Conflict.* New York: Free Press.

Crandall, Robert. 1986. "The Transformation of U.S. Manufacturing." *Industrial Relations* 25:118-30.

Cutler, David and Lawrence Katz. 1992. "Rising Income Inequality: Changes in the Distribution of Income and Consumption in the '80s." *American Economic Review* 82:541-52.

Cyret, Richard M. and James G. March. 1963. *A Behavioral Theory of the Firm.* Englewood Cliffs, NJ: Prentice Hall.

Davidson, William H. and Phillipe Haspaugh. 1982. "Shaping a Global Product Organization." *Harvard Business Review* 60:125-32.

Davis, Gerald F., Kristina A. Diekmann, and Catherine H. Tinsley. 1994. "The Decline and Fall of the Conglomerate Firm." *American Sociological Review* 59:547-70.

Davis, Stephen. 1992. "Cross-Country Patterns of Change in Relative Wages." Pp. 239-300 in *National Bureau of Economic Research Macroeconomics Annual, 1992.* Cambridge: MIT Press.

Dean, Edwin, Harry Boissevain, and James Thomas. 1986. "Productivity and Labor Cost Trends in Manufacturing, 12 Countries." *Monthly Labor Review* 109:3-10.

Deane, Phyllis. 1965. *The First Industrial Revolution.* London: Cambridge University Press.

Demone, Harold, Jr. and Margaret Gibleman. 1987. "Privatizing the Acute Care General Hospital." Pp. 50-75 in *Private Means, Public Ends,* edited by Barry J. Carroll, Ralph Conant, and Thomas Easton. Westport, CT: Praeger.

Dickens, William. 1983. "The Effect of Company Campaigns on Union Certification Elections: Law and Reality Once Again." *International Labor Relations Review* 36:560-75.

Dickens, William and Jonathan Leonard. 1985. "Accounting for the Decline in Union Membership, 1950-1980." *International Labor Relations Review* 38:323-34.

DiMaggio, Paul and Walter Powell. 1983. "Institutional Isomorphism." *American Sociological Review* 48:147-60.

Dollar, David and Edward Wolfe. 1988. "Convergence of Industry Labor Productivity Among Advanced Economies, 1963-82." *Review of Economics and Statistics* 70:549-58.

Downs, George and Patrick Larkey. 1986. *The Search for Government Efficiency.* Philadelphia: Temple University Press.

Drucker, Peter. 1964. *Managing for Results*. New York: Harper and Row.

Drucker, Peter. 1974. *Management*. New York: Harper and Row.

Drucker, Peter. 1992. "The Economy's Power Shift." *The Wall Street Journal*, September 24, p. A16.

Eccles, Robert and Dwight Crane. 1988. *Doing Deals: Investment Banks at Work*. Boston: Harvard Business School Press.

Eccles, Robert G. and Nitin Nohria (with James Berkley). 1992. *Beyond the Hype: Rediscovering the Essence of Management*. Cambridge, MA: Harvard Business School Press.

Edsall, Thomas. 1984. *The New Politics of Inequality*. New York: Norton.

Edsall, Thomas. 1989. "The Changing Shape of Power: A Realignment in Public Policy." Pp. 269-93 in *The Rise and Fall of the New Deal Order*, edited by Steve Fraser and Gary Gerstle. Princeton, NJ: Princeton University Press.

Edwards, Richard. 1979. *Contested Terrain: The Transformation of the Workplace in the Twentieth Century*. New York: Basic Books.

Egelhoff, William. 1988. "Strategy and Structure in Multinational Corporations: A Revision of the Stopford and Wells Model." *Strategic Management Journal* 9:1-14.

Elster, John. 1983. *Explaining Technical Change*. Cambridge: Cambridge University Press.

Eulau, Heinz and Michael Lewis-Beck. 1985. *Economic Conditions and Electoral Outcomes*. New York: Agathon Press.

Evans, Peter. 1981. "Recent Research in Multinational Corporations." *Annual Review of Sociology* 7:199-233.

Fantasia, Rick, Dan Clawson, and Gregory Graham. 1988. "A Critical View of Worker Participation in American Industry." *Work and Occupations* 15:468-88.

Farber, Henry. 1987. "The Recent Decline in Unionization in the United States." *Science* 238:915-20.

Fenneman, Mernder and Kees van der Pijl. 1987. "International Bank Capital and the New Liberalism." Pp. 298-319 in *The Structural Analysis of Business*, edited by Mark Mizruchi and Michael Schwartz. Cambridge: Cambridge University Press.

Ferguson, Thomas and Joel Rogers. 1986. *Right Turn: The Decline of the Democrats and the Future of American Politics*. New York: Hill and Wang.

Fiorito, Jack, Christopher Lowman, and Forrest Nelson. 1987. "The Impact of Human Resource Policies on Union Organizing." *Industrial Relations* 26:113-26.

Fligstein, Neil. 1990. *The Transformation of Corporate Control*. Cambridge, MA: Harvard University Press.

Flood, Ann and W. Richard Scott. 1987. *Hospital Structure and Performance*. Baltimore: The Johns Hopkins University Press.

Foulkes, Fred. 1980. *Personnel Policies in Large Nonunion Companies*. Englewood Cliffs, NJ: Prentice Hall.

Franko, Lawrence G. 1991. "Global Corporate Competition: Is the Large American Firm an Endangered Species?" *Business Horizons* 34:14-22.

Freeman, Richard. 1985. "Why Are Workers Faring Poorly in NLRB Representation Elections?" Pp. 45-64 in *Challenges and Choices Facing American Labor*, edited by Thomas Kochan. Cambridge: MIT Press.

Freeman, Richard. 1986. "In Search of Union Wage Concessions in Standard Data Sets." *Industrial Relations* 25:131-45.

Freeman, Richard and James Medoff. 1984. *What Do Unions Do?* New York: Basic Books.

Freidson, Eliot. 1984. "The Changing Nature of Professional Control." *Annual Review of Sociology* 10:1-20.

Friedland, Roger and Robert Alford. 1991. "Bringing Society Back In: Symbols, Practices, and Institutional Contradictions." Pp. 232-63 *The New Institutionalism in*

Organizational Analysis, edited by Walter W. Powell and Paul J. DiMaggio. Chicago: University of Chicago Press.

Fröbel, Folker, Jürgen Heinrichs, and Otto Kreye. 1980. *The New International Division of Labor*. London: Cambridge University Press.

Galbraith, John. 1967. *New Industrial State*. Boston: Houghton Mifflin.

General Accounting Office. 1986. *Public Hospitals*. Washington, DC: Office of Public Information.

General Accounting Office. 1987. *Plant Closings: Limited Advance Notice and Assistance Provided Dislocated Workers*. Washington, DC: General Accounting Office.

Gershenfeld, Walter J. 1987. "Employee Participation in Firm Decisions." Pp. 123-58 in *Human Resources and the Performance of Firms*, edited by Morris Kleiner. Madison: Industrial Relations Association, University of Wisconsin.

Ghoshal, Sumantra and Christopher Bartlett. 1990. "The Multinational Corporation as an International Network." *Academy of Management Review* 15:603-25.

Ghoshal, Sumantra and Nitin Nohria. 1993. "Horses for Courses: Organizational Forms for Multinational Corporations." *Sloan Management Review* 34:23-36.

Giddens, Anthony. 1990. *The Consequences of Modernity*. Stanford, CA: Stanford University Press.

Gilbert, Neil. 1983. *Capitalism and the Welfare State*. New Haven, CT: Yale University Press.

Gilbert, Neil and Harry Sprecht. 1986. *Dimensions of Social Welfare Policy*. Englewood Cliffs, NJ: Prentice Hall.

Ginzberg, Eli. 1990. *The Medical Triangle*. Cambridge, MA: Harvard University Press.

Goldthorpe, John. 1984. "The End of Convergence: Corporatist and Dualist Tendencies in Modern Western Societies." Pp. 315-43 in *Order and Conflict in Contemporary Capitalism*, edited by John Goldthorpe. New York: Oxford University Press.

Gordon, David, Richard Edwards, and Michael Reich. 1982. *Segmented Work, Divided Workers: The Historical Transformation of Labor in the United States*. Cambridge: Cambridge University Press.

Gouldner, Alvin. 1970. *The Coming Crisis of Western Sociology*. New York: Basic Books.

Gramlich, Edward and Patricia Koshel. 1975. *Educational Performance Contracting*. Washington, DC: The Brookings Institution.

Granovetter, Mark. 1984. "Small Is Bountiful: Labor Markets and Establishment Size." *American Sociological Review* 49:323-34.

Gray, Bradford. 1986. *For-Profit Enterprise in Health Care*. Washington, DC: National Academy Press.

Greenfield, Harry. 1966. *Manpower and the Growth of Producer Services*. New York: Columbia University Press.

Grenier, Guillermo. 1988. *Inhuman Relations: Quality Circles and Anti-Unionism in American Industry*. Philadelphia: Temple University Press.

Grenier, Guillermo and Raymond Hogler. 1991. "Labor Law and Managerial Ideology." *Work and Occupations* 18:313-33.

Griffin, Larry, Michael Wallace, and Beth Rubin. 1986. "Capitalist Resistance to the Organization of Labor Before the New Deal." *American Sociological Review* 51:147-67.

Grinyer, Peter, Peter McKieran, and Yasai-Ardeki Masoud. 1988. "Market, Organizational and Managerial Correlates of Economic Performance in the U.K. Electrical Engineering Industry." *Strategic Management Journal* 9:297-318.

Grubb, W. Norton and Robert Wilson. 1989. "Sources of Increasing Inequality in Wages and Salaries, 1960-80." *Monthly Labor Review* 112:3-13.

Gurin, Arnold. 1989. "Governmental Responsibility and Privatization." Pp. 179-205 in *Privatization and the Welfare State*, edited by Sheila Kamerman and Alfred Kahn. Princeton, NJ: Princeton University Press.

Gurin, Arnold and B. Friedman. 1981. "Contracting for Services as a Mechanism for the Delivery of Human Services." Brandeis: Florence Heller Graduate School for Advanced Studies in Social Welfare.

Hage, Jerald. 1988. *The Futures of Organizations*. Lexington, MA: D. C. Heath.

Hannan, Michael and John Freeman. 1989. *Organizational Ecology*. Cambridge, MA: Harvard University Press.

Hannaway, Jane. 1987. "Supply Creates Demand." *Journal of Policy Analysis and Management* 7:118-34.

Hansen, Gary and Birger Wernerfelt. 1989. "Determinants of Firm Performance: The Relative Importance of Economic and Organizational Factors." *Strategic Management Journal* 10:399-411.

Harrington, Michael. 1976. "Post-Industrial Society and the Welfare State." *Dissent* 23:244-52.

Harrison, Bennett and Barry Bluestone. 1988. *The Great U-Turn: Corporate Restructuring and the Polarizing of America*. New York: Basic Books.

Hasenfeld, Yeheskel. 1984. "The Changing Context of Human Services Administration." *Social Work* 29:522-29.

Hasenfeld, Yeheskel. 1985. "Citizens' Encounters with Welfare State Bureaucracies." *Social Science Review* 59:622-35.

Hawes, Catherine and Charles Phillips. 1986. "The Changing Structure of the Nursing Home Industry and the Impact of Ownership on Quality, Cost, and Care." Pp. 492-541 in *For-Profit Enterprise in Health Care*, edited by Bradford Gray. Washington, DC: National Academy Press.

Hawkins, Robert and Ingo Walter. 1981. "Planning Multinational Operations." Pp. 253-67 in *Handbook of Organizational Design*, edited by Paul Nystrom and William Starbuck. New York: Oxford University Press.

Hawley, Amos. 1968. "Human Ecology." Pp. 328-37 in *International Encyclopedia of the Social Sciences*, Vol. 4, edited by David Sills. New York: Macmillan and Free Press.

Heckscher, Charles C. 1988. *The New Unionism: Employee Involvement in the Corporation*. New York: Basic Books.

Heilbroner, Robert and Aaron Singer. 1984. *The Economic Transformation of America*. New York: Harcourt, Brace, Jovanovich.

Henderson, John and N. Venkatraman. 1992. "Strategic Alignment: A Model for Organizational Transformation Through Information Technology." Pp. 97-116 in *Transforming Organizations*, edited by Thomas A. Kochan and Michael Useem. New York: Oxford University Press.

Herman, Edward S. 1981. *Corporate Control, Corporate Power*. New York: Cambridge University Press.

Heydebrand, Wolf. 1983. "Technocratic Corporatism: Toward a Theory of Occupational and Organizational Transformation." Pp. 93-114 in *Organizational Theory and Public Policy*, edited by Richard Hall and Robert Quinn. Beverly Hills, CA: Sage.

Heydebrand, Wolf. 1989. "New Organizational Forms." *Work and Occupations* 16:323-57.

Hill, Charles and Peter Hwang. 1990. "An Eclectic Theory of the Choice of International Entry Mode." *Strategic Management Journal* 11:117-28.

Himmelstein, Jerome. 1990. *To The Right: The Transformation of American Conservatism*. Berkeley: University of California Press.

Himmelstein, Jerome and James McRae. 1988. "Social Issues and SES." *Public Opinion Quarterly* 52:492-512.

Hofstadter, Richard. 1973. *The American Political Tradition and the Men Who Made It*. New York: Knopf.

Hollander, Stanley and Glenn Omura. 1989. "Chain Store Developments and Their Political, Strategic, and Social Interdependencies." *Journal of Retailing* 65:299-325.

Hopkins, Terrance. 1982. "The Study of the Capitalist World Economy: Some Introductory Considerations." Pp. 9-38 in *World Systems Analysis: Theory and Methodology*, edited by Terrance Hopkins et al. Beverly Hills, CA: Sage.

Hout, Thomas M., Michael Porter, and Eileen Rudden. 1982. "How Global Companies Win Out." *Harvard Business Review* 60:98-108.

Hughes, H. Stuart and James Wilkinson. 1987. *Contemporary Europe: A History*. Englewood Cliffs, NJ: Prentice Hall.

Hull, Frank and Koya Azumi. 1988. "Technology and Participation in Japanese Factories." *Work and Occupations* 15:423-48.

Hymer, Stephen. 1971. "The Multinational Corporation and the Law of Uneven Development." Pp. 113-40 in *Economics and World Order*, edited by J. W. Bhagwati. New York: World Law Fund.

Inglehart, Ronald. 1984. "The Changing Structure of Political Cleavages in Western Society." Pp. 25-69 in *Electoral Change in Advanced Industrial Democracies*, edited by Russell Dalton, Scott Flanagan, and Paul Beck. Princeton, NJ: Princeton University Press.

Inglehart, Ronald. 1986. "Intergenerational Changes in Politics and Culture." Pp. 81-105 in *Research in Political Sociology*, Vol. 2, edited by Richard Braungart and Margaret Braungart. Greenwich, CT: JAI Press.

Jacobs, David, Michael Useem, and Mayer Zald. 1991. "Firms, Industries, and Politics." Pp. 141-65 in *Research in Political Sociology*, Vol. 5, edited by Philo Wasburn. Greenwich, CT: JAI Press.

Jameson, Frederic. 1971. *Marxism and Form: Twentieth-Century Dialectical Theories of Literature*. Princeton, NJ: Princeton University Press.

Jencks, Christopher. 1985. "How Much Do High School Students Learn?" *Sociology of Education* 58:128-35.

Jencks, Christopher. 1992. *Rethinking Social Policy: Race, Poverty, and the Underclass*. Cambridge, MA: Harvard University Press.

Kalleberg, Arne L., Michael Wallace, and Robert P. Althauser. 1981. "Economic Segmentation, Worker Power, and Income Inequality." *American Journal of Sociology* 87:651-83.

Kamerman, Sheila and Alfred Kahn. 1989. "Child Care and Privatization under Reagan." Pp. 235-59 in *Privatization and the Welfare State*, edited by Sheila Kamerman and Alfred Kahn. Princeton, NJ: Princeton University Press.

Kanter, Rosabeth. 1983. *The Change Masters*. New York: Simon and Schuster.

Katz, Harry, Thomas Kochan, and Kenneth Gobeille. 1983. "Industrial Relations Performance and QWL Programs." *International Labor Relations Review* 37:3-17.

Kerr, Clark, John Dunlop, Frederick Harbison, and Charles Myers. 1964. *Industrialism and Industrial Man* (2nd ed.). New York: Oxford University Press.

Kochan, Thomas. 1980. *Collective Bargaining and Industrial Relations*. Homewood, IL: Richard D. Irwin.

Kochan, Thomas and Peter Cappelli. 1984. "The Transformation of the Industrial Relations and Personnel Function." Pp. 133-61 in *Internal Labor Markets*, edited by Paul Osterman. Cambridge: MIT Press.

Kochan, Thomas, Harry Katz, and Robert McKersie. 1986. *The Transformation of American Industrial Relations*. New York: Basic Books.

Kochan, Thomas, Robert McKersie, and John Chalykoff. 1986. "The Effects of Corporate Strategy and Workplace Innovations on Union Representation." *International Labor Relations Review* 39:487-501.

Kochan, Thomas and Michael Useem. 1992. *Transforming Organizations*. New York: Oxford University Press.

Kolson, Kenneth. 1982. "Management and Higher Learning." *Liberal Education* 68:211-19.

Kravis, Irving. 1985. "Services in World Transactions." Pp. 135-60 in *Managing the Service Economy: Prospects and Problems*, edited by Robert Inman. Cambridge: Cambridge University Press.

Kravis, Irving, Alan Heston, and Robert Summers. 1983. "The Share of Services in Economic Growth." Pp. 188-218 in *Global Econometrics*, edited by F. Gerard Adams and Bert Hickman. Cambridge: MIT Press.

Krugman, Paul. 1994. "Competitiveness: A Dangerous Obsession." *Foreign Affairs Quarterly* 73:28-44.

Krugman, Paul R. and Robert Z. Lawrence. 1994. "Trade, Jobs, and Wages." *Scientific American* 270:44-49.

Kutscher, Ronald and Valerie Personick. 1986. "Deindustrialization and the Shift to Services." *Monthly Labor Review* 109:3-13.

Kuznets, Simon. 1955. "Economic Growth and Income Inequality." *American Economic Review* 45:1-28.

Lampman, Robert. 1962. *The Share of Top Wealth-Holders in National Wealth*. Princeton, NJ: Princeton University Press.

Lane, Robert. 1986. "Market Justice, Political Justice." *American Political Science Review* 80:383-402.

Lash, Scott and John Urry. 1987. *The End of Organized Capitalism*. Madison: University of Wisconsin Press.

Laumann, Edward and John Heinz. 1985. "Washington Lawyers and Others." *Stanford Law Review* 37:465-502.

Lawler, John. 1982. "Labor-Management Consultants in Union Organizing Campaigns." Pp. 374-80 in *Proceedings of the 34th Annual Meeting of the Industrial Relations Association*. Madison: Industrial Relations Research Association, University of Wisconsin.

Lawler, John. 1986. "Union Growth and Decline: The Impact of Employer and Union Tactics." *Journal of Occupational Psychology* 59:217-30.

Lawrence, Robert Z. and Matthew J. Slaughter. 1993. "Trade and U.S. Wages: Giant Sucking Sound or Small Hiccup?" *Brookings Papers on Economic Activity* 2:161-210.

Lawrence, S., R. A. Derzon, and R. Margulies. 1981. "Investor-Owned and Nonprofits Differ in Economic Performance." *Hospitals* 55:52-58.

Leavitt, Theodore. 1986. *The Marketing Imagination*. New York: Free Press.

Lenski, Gerhard. 1966. *Power and Privilege*. New York: McGraw-Hill.

Levich, Richard and Ingo Walter. 1990. "The Regulation of Global Financial Markets." Pp. 51-89 in *New York's Financial Markets*, edited by Thierry Noyelle. Boulder, CO: Westview Press.

Levy, Frank. 1988. *Dollars and Dreams: The Changing American Income Distribution*. New York: Russell Sage.

Lewis, H. Gregg. 1963. *Unionism and Relative Wages in the United States*. Chicago: University of Chicago Press.

Lewis, Sinclair. 1945. *Arrowsmith*. New York: Harcourt Brace.

Light, Donald. 1986. "Surplus vs. Cost Containment: The Changing Context for Health Providers." Pp. 519-42 in *Applications of Social Science to Clinical Medicine and Health Policy*, edited by Linda Aiken and David Mechanic. New Brunswick, NJ: Rutgers University Press.

Lindberg, Gregory L., Nicole Lurie, and Susan Bannick-Mohrland. 1989. "Health Care Cost Containment Measures and Mortality in Hennepin County's Medicaid Elderly and All Elderly." *American Journal of Public Health* 79:1481-85.

Lipset, Seymour. 1960. *Political Man*. New York: Doubleday.

Lipset, Seymour. 1968. *Revolution and Counterrevolution*. New York: Basic Books.

Lipset, Seymour. 1986. "North American Labor Movements: A Comparative Perspective." Pp. 421-52 in *Unions in Transition*, edited by Seymour Lipset. San Francisco: ICS Press.

Lipset, Seymour and William Schneider. 1987. *The Confidence Gap: Business, Labor, and Government in the Public Mind*. Baltimore: The Johns Hopkins University Press.

Locke, Robert. 1989. *Management and Higher Education Since 1940: The Influence of America and Japan on West Germany, Great Britain, and France*. New York: Cambridge University Press.

Lorence, Jon and Joel I. Nelson. 1993. "Industrial Restructuring and Metropolitan Earnings Inequality: 1970-1980." *Research in Social Stratification and Mobility* 12: 145-84.

Luttwak, Edward. 1993. *The Endangered American Dream: How to Stop the United States from Becoming a Third World Country and How to Win the Geo-Economic Struggle for Industrial Supremacy*. New York: Simon and Schuster.

Luttwak, Edward. 1994. "Why Facism Is the Wave of the Future." *London Review of Books* 16(April 7):3, 5.

Mandel, Ernest. 1976. *Late Capitalism*, translated by Joris De Bres. London: NLB.

March, James and Herbert Simon. 1958. *Organizations*. New York: John Wiley.

Marshall, T. H. 1965. *Class, Citizenship, and Social Development*. Garden City, NY: Doubleday.

Marx, Karl. 1936. *Capital*. New York: Modern Library.

Maxwell, Nan. 1989. "Demographic and Economic Determinants of United States Income Inequality." *Social Science Quarterly* 70:243-64.

Mayer, Kurt B. and Sydney Goldstein. 1961. *The First Two Years: Problems of Small Firm Growth and Survival*. Washington, DC: Small Business Administration.

McCarthy, John and Mayer Zald. 1977. "Resource Mobilization and Social Movements." *American Journal of Sociology* 82:1212-41.

McCracken, Grant. 1988. *Culture and Consumption*. Bloomington: University of Indiana Press.

Meyer, John and Brian Rowan. 1977. "Institutionalized Organizations: Formal Structure as Myth and Ceremony." *American Journal of Sociology* 83:340-63.

Miller, Danny. 1986. "Configurations of Strategy and Structure: Toward a Synthesis." *Strategic Management Journal* 7:233-49.

Mills, C. Wright. 1951. *White Collar*. New York: Oxford University Press.

Minsky, Hyman. 1986. *Stabilizing an Unstable Economy*. New Haven, CT: Yale University Press.

Mizruchi, Mark. 1992. *The Structure of Corporate Political Action: Interfirm Relations and Their Consequences*. Cambridge, MA: Harvard University Press.

Montagna, Paul. 1990. "Accounting Rationality and Financial Legitimation." Pp. 227-60 in *Structures of Capital*, edited by Sharon Zukin and Paul DiMaggio. Cambridge: Cambridge University Press.

Morlock, Edward and Philip Vitton. 1985. "The Comparative Costs of Public and Private Providers of Mass Transit." Pp. 233-54 in *Urban Transit: The Private Challenge to Public Transportation*, edited by Charles Lave. Cambridge, MA: Ballinger.

Murrimann, Kent and Andrew Porter. 1982. "Employer Campaign Tactics and NLRB Election Outcomes." Pp. 67-72 in *Proceedings of the 35th Annual Meeting of the Industrial Relations Association*. Madison: Industrial Relations Research Association, University of Wisconsin.

Nelson, Daniel. 1975. *Managers and Workers: Origins of the New Factory System in the United States*. Madison: University of Wisconsin Press.

Nelson, Joel. 1981. *Economic Inequality: Conflict Without Change.* New York: Columbia University Press.

Nelson, Joel and Jon Lorence. 1988. "Metropolitan Earnings Inequality and Service Sector Employment." *Social Forces* 67:492-511.

Nelson, Richard and Sidney Winter. 1982. *An Evolutionary Theory of Economic Change.* Cambridge, MA: Harvard University Press.

New York Times. 1990. "Unequal Pay Widespread in U.S." August 14, pp. D1, D8.

New York Times. 1991. "American Revival in Manufacturing Seen in U.S. Report." February 5, pp. A1 and C17.

New York Times. 1992a. "Fed Gives New Evidence of '80s Gains by Richest Households." April 21, pp. A1, A6.

New York Times. 1992b. "The 1980's: A Very Good Time for the Rich." March 5, p. A1.

New York Times. 1992c. "Report Delayed Months, Says Lowest Income Group Grew Sharply." May 12, p. A7.

New York Times. 1992d. "Research Questions Effectiveness of Most School Choice." October 26, p. A1.

New York Times. 1992e. "The Rich Get Richer, But Never the Same Way." August 16, p. E3.

New York Times. 1992f. "U.S. Rate of Output Called Best." October 13, pp. C1, C16.

New York Times. 1994. "Male, Educated, and in a Pay Bind." February 11, pp. C1, C4.

Nielsen, François. 1994. "Income Inequality and Industrial Development." *American Sociological Review* 59:654-77.

Nohria, Nitin and James D. Berkley. 1994. "Whatever Happened to the Take-Charge Manager?" *Harvard Business Review* 72:128-37.

Norsworthy, J. R. and Craig Zabala. 1985. "Worker Attitudes, Worker Behavior, and Productivity in the U.S. Automobile Industry." *International Labor Relations Review* 38:544-57.

Noyelle, Thierry. 1988. *International Trade in Business Services.* Cambridge, MA: Ballinger.

Nye, Joseph. 1990. *Bound to Lead: The Changing Nature of American Power.* New York: Basic Books.

O'Connor, James. 1973. *The Fiscal Crisis of the State.* New York: St. Martin's.

Ochel, Wolfgang and Manfred Wegner. 1987. *Service Economies in Europe.* Boulder, CO: Westview Press.

Okun, Arthur. 1975. *Equality and Efficiency.* Washington, DC: The Brookings Institution.

Olson, Mancur. 1965. *The Logic of Collective Action.* Cambridge, MA: Harvard University Press.

Oster, Sharon. 1990. *Modern Competitive Analysis.* New York: Oxford University Press.

Osterman, Paul. 1988. *Employment Futures: Reorganization, Dislocation, and Public Policy.* New York: Oxford University Press.

Pack, Janet. 1987. "Privatization of Public Sector Services in Theory and Practice." *Journal of Policy Analysis and Management* 6:523-40.

Parcel, Toby and Marie Sickmeier. 1988. "One Firm, Two Labor Markets: The Case of McDonald's in the Fast-Food Industry." *Sociological Quarterly* 29:29-46.

Parsons, Talcott. 1951. *The Social System.* Glencoe, IL: Free Press.

Parsons, Talcott. 1960. *Structure and Process in Modern Society.* Glencoe, IL: Free Press.

Patton, Michael. 1982. *Practical Evaluation.* Beverly Hills, CA: Sage.

Peacock, Walter, Greg Hoover, and Charles Killian. 1988. "Divergence and Convergence in International Development." *American Sociological Review* 53:838-52.

Perrow, Charles. 1970. "Demystifying Organizations." Pp. 105-20 in *The Management of Human Services,* edited by Rosemary Sarri and Yeheskel Hasenfeld. New York: Columbia University Press.

Pescheck, Joseph. 1987. *Policy Planning Organizations*. Philadelphia: Temple University Press.

Peters, B. Guy. 1973. "Equality in Sweden and the United Kingdom: A Longitudinal Analysis." *Acta Sociologica* 16:108-20.

Peters, Thomas and Robert Waterman. 1982. *In Search of Excellence*. New York: Harper and Row.

Pfeffer, Jeffrey. 1987. "A Resource Dependence Perspective on Intercorporate Relations." Pp. 25-55 in *The Structural Analysis of Business*, edited by Mark Mizruchi and Michael Schwartz. Cambridge: Cambridge University Press.

Pfeffer, Jeffrey and Alison Davis-Blake. 1990. "Unions and Job Satisfaction." *Work and Occupations* 17:259-83.

Phillips, Kevin. 1990. *The Politics of Rich and Poor: Wealth and the American Electorate in the Reagan Aftermath*. New York: Random House.

Piore, Michael and Charles Sabel. 1984. *The Second Industrial Divide: Possibilities for Prosperity*. New York: Basic Books.

Polanyi, Karl. 1957. *The Great Transformation*. Boston: Beacon.

Poole, Robert. 1983. "Objections to Privatization." *Policy Review* 24:105-19.

Poole, Robert and Philip Fixler. 1987. "Privatization and Public Sector Services in Practice: Experiences and Potential." *Journal of Policy and Management Review* 6:612-25.

Porter, Lyman and Lawrence McKibbin. 1988. *Management Education and Development: Drift or Thrust Into the 21st Century?* New York: McGraw-Hill.

Porter, Michael. 1985. *Competitive Advantage*. New York: Free Press.

Porter, Michael. 1988. *Competitive Strategy: Techniques for Analyzing Industries and Competitors*. New York: Free Press.

Post, James, Edwin Murray, Jr., Robert Dickie, and John Mahon. 1983. "Managing Public Affairs." *California Management Review* 26:135-50.

Powell, Walter. 1990. "Neither Markets Nor Hierarchy: Network Forms of Organization." Pp. 295-336 in *Research in Organizational Behavior*, Vol. 12, edited by Barry Staw and L. L. Cummings. Greenwich, CT: JAI Press.

Powell, Walter W. and Paul J. DiMaggio, eds. 1991. *The New Institutionalism in Organizational Analysis*. Chicago: University of Chicago Press.

Prescott, John, Ajay Kohli, and N. Venkatraman. 1986. "The Market Share-Profitability Relationship: An Empirical Assessment of Major Assertions and Contradictions." *Strategic Management Journal* 7:377-94.

Prinsky, Lorraine. 1978. "Public vs. Private: Organizational Control as Determinant of Administrative Size." *Sociology and Social Research* 62:401-13.

Prottas, Jeffrey. 1979. *People Processing*. Lexington, MA: D. C. Heath.

Przeworski, Adam. 1985. *Capitalism and Social Democracy*. New York: Cambridge University Press.

Quinn, James. 1988. "Technology in Services." *Technological Forecasting and Social Change* 34:327-50.

Reich, Robert. 1981. "Regulation by Confrontation or Negotiation." *Harvard Business Review* 59:82-93.

Reich, Robert. 1984. *The Next American Frontier*. Middlesex, UK: Harmondsworth.

Revenga, Ana. 1992. "Exporting Jobs: The Impact of Import Completion on Employment and Wages in U.S. Manufacturing." *Quarterly Journal of Economics* 107:225-84.

Reynolds, Morgan and Eugene Smolensky. 1977. *Public Expenditures, Taxes, and the Distribution of Income in the United States: 1950, 1961, 1970*. New York: Academic Press.

Riche, Richard, Daniel Hecker, and John Burgan. 1983. "High Technology Today and Tomorrow: A Small Slice of the Employment Pie." *Monthly Labor Review* 106:50-58.

Ross, Robert and Kent Trachte. 1990. *Global Capitalism: The New Leviathan.* Albany: SUNY Press.

Rubin, Paul H. 1973. "The Expansion of Firms." *Journal of Political Economy* 81:936-49.

Rubin, Paul H. 1978. "The Theory of the Firm and the Structure of the Franchise Contract." *Journal of Law and Economics* 21:223-34.

Sabato, Larry. 1981. *The Rise of Political Consultants.* New York: Basic Books.

Sabato, Larry. 1984. *Pac Power.* New York: Norton.

Sachs, Jeffrey and Howard J. Shatz. 1994. "Trade and Jobs in U.S. Manufacturing." *Brookings Papers on Economic Activity,* 1-84.

Sappington, David and Joseph Stiglitz. 1987. "Privatization, Information, and Incentives." *Journal of Policy Analysis and Management* 6:567-82.

Sassen, Saskia. 1990. "Economic Restructuring and the American City." *Annual Review of Sociology* 16:465-90.

Savas, Emanuel S. 1977a. *Alternatives for Delivering Public Services.* Boulder, CO: Westview Press.

Savas, Emanuel S. 1977b. *The Organization and Efficiency of Solid Waste Collection.* Lexington, MA: Lexington Books.

Schlesinger, Mark, Robert Dorwat, and Richard Pulice. 1986. "Competitive Bidding and States' Purchase of Services: The Case of Mental Health in Massachusetts." *Journal of Policy Analysis and Management* 5:245-63.

Schlozman, Kay. 1984. "What Accent the Heavenly Chorus? Political Equality and the American Pressure System." *Journal of Politics* 46:1006-32.

Schlozman, Kay and John Tierney. 1983. "More of the Same: Pressure Group Activity in a Decade of Change." *Journal of Politics* 45:351-75.

Schumpeter, Joseph. 1934. *The Theory of Economic Development.* Cambridge, MA: Harvard University Press.

Schumpeter, Joseph. 1939. *Business Cycles.* New York: McGraw-Hill.

Schumpeter, Joseph. [1942] 1961. *Capitalism, Socialism, and Democracy.* London: George Allen and Unwin.

Scott, W. Richard. 1992. *Organizations: Rational, Natural, and Open Systems.* Englewood Cliffs, NJ: Prentice Hall.

Scott, W. Richard and John W. Meyer. 1991. "The Organization of Societal Sectors: Propositions and Early Evidence." Pp. 108-40 in *The New Institutionalism in Organizational Analysis,* edited by Walter W. Powell and Paul J. DiMaggio. Chicago: University of Chicago Press.

Scott Morton, Michael S. 1991. *The Corporation of the 1990s.* New York: Oxford University Press.

Shonick, William and Ruth Roemer. 1982. *Private Management of California State Hospitals.* Los Angeles: School of Public Health, University of California at Los Angeles.

Shorrocks, A. F. 1987. "U.K. Wealth Distribution: Current Evidence and Future Prospects." Pp. 72-89 in *International Comparisons of the Distribution of Household Wealth,* edited by Edward Wolff. New York: Oxford University Press.

Silk, Leonard and David Vogel. 1976. *Ethics and Profits: The Crisis of Confidence in American Business.* New York: Simon and Schuster.

Simon, Herbert. 1957. *Administrative Behavior.* New York: Macmillan.

Sjoberg, Gideon and Richard Brymer. 1966. "Bureaucracy and the Lower Class." *Sociology and Social Research* 50:325-37.

Smith, James D. 1984. "Trends in Personal Wealth in the United States, 1958-1976." *Review of Income and Wealth* (Series 30):419-28.

Smith, Roy. 1990. "International Stock Market Transactions." Pp. 7-29 in *New York's Financial Markets,* edited by Thierry Noyelle. Boulder, CO: Westview Press.

Soltow, Lee. 1965. *Toward Income Equality in Norway*. Madison: University of Wisconsin Press.

Soltow, Lee. 1968. "Long-Run Changes in British Income Inequality." *Economic History Review* 21:17-29.

Soltow, Lee. 1971. *Patterns of Wealthholding in Wisconsin since 1850*. Madison: University of Wisconsin Press.

Soltow, Lee. 1975. *Man and Wealth in the United States, 1850-1870*. New Haven, CT: Yale University Press.

Sorokin, Pitirim. 1937. *Social and Cultural Dynamics*. New York: American Book Company.

Spant, Roland. 1987. "Wealth Distribution in Sweden." Pp. 51-71 in *International Comparisons of the Distribution of Household Wealth*, edited by Edward Wolff. New York: Oxford University Press.

Spengler, Oswald. 1926. *The Decline of the West*. New York: Knopf.

Stanback, Thomas. 1979. *Understanding the Service Economy*. Baltimore: The Johns Hopkins University Press.

Stanback, Thomas, Peter Bearse, Thierry Noyelle, and Robert Karasek. 1981. *Services: A New Economy*. Totowa, NJ: Allanheld, Osman.

Starr, Paul. 1982. *The Social Transformation of American Medicine*. New York: Basic Books.

Starr, Paul. 1989. "The Meaning of Privatization." Pp. 15-48 in *Privatization and the Welfare State*, edited by Sheila Kamerman and Alfred Kahn. Princeton, NJ: Princeton University Press.

Stiglitz, Joseph. 1988. *Economics of the Public Sector*. New York: Norton.

Stinchcombe, Arthur. 1961. "Agricultural Enterprise and Rural Class Relations." *American Journal of Sociology* 67:165-76.

Stinchcombe, Arthur. 1990. *Information and Organizations*. Berkeley: University of California Press.

Stoesz, David. 1986. "Corporate Welfare: The 3rd Stage of Welfare in the U.S." *Social Work* 31:245-49.

Stopford, John and Louis Wells, Jr. 1972. *Managing the Multinational Enterprise*. New York: Basic Books.

Strauss, George. 1984. "Industrial Relations: Time of Change." *Industrial Relations* 23:1-15.

Straussman, Jeffrey. 1981. "Contracting for Social Services at the Local Level." *Urban Interest* 3:43-50.

Suchman, Mark. 1992. "On Advice of Counsel: Law Firms as Information Intermediaries in the Structuration of Silicon Valley." Paper presented to the Sociology Department, University of Minnesota, Minneapolis, MN, January 27.

Summers, Robert. 1985. "Services in the International Economy." Pp. 27-48 in *Managing the Service Economy: Prospects and Problems*, edited by Robert Inman. Cambridge: Cambridge University Press.

Tausky, Curt and Anthony Chelter. 1988. "Workers' Participation." *Work and Occupations* 15:363-73.

Taylor, Charles and Gail Fosler. 1994. "The Necessity of Being Global." *Across the Board: The Conference Board Magazine* 31:40-43.

Taylor, William. 1991. "The Logic of Global Business: An Interview with ABB's Percy Barnevik." *Harvard Business Review* 49:91-105.

Thompson, James. 1967. *Organizations in Action*. New York: McGraw-Hill.

Thrift, Nigel. 1987. "The Fixers: The Urban Geography of International Commercial Capital." Pp. 201-33 in *Global Restructuring and Territorial Development*, edited by Jeffrey Henderson and Manuel Castells. Newbury Park, CA: Sage.

Titmuss, Richard. 1963. *Essays on "The Welfare State."* London: Unwin University Books.

Toynbee, Arnold. 1935. *A Study of History.* London: Oxford University Press.

Troy, Leo. 1986. "The Rise and Fall of American Trade Unions." Pp. 75-109 in *Unions in Transition*, edited by Seymour Lipset. San Francisco: ICS Press.

Tsurumi, Yoshi. 1984. *Multinational Management: Business Strategy and Government Policy.* Cambridge, MA: Ballinger.

Tushman, M. and D. Nadler. 1986. "Organizing for Innovation." *California Management Review* 28:74-92.

Udy, Stanley. 1958. " 'Bureaucratic' Elements in Organizations: Some Research Findings." *American Sociological Review* 23:415-20.

U.S. Bureau of the Census. 1943. *16th Census of the United States, 1940.* Volume 3, *Occupation, Industry, Employment and Income.* Washington, DC: Government Printing Office.

U. S. Bureau of the Census. 1976. *Census of Retail Trade, 1972.* Volume 1, *Summary and Subject Statistics.* Washington, DC: Government Printing Office.

U. S. Bureau of the Census. 1977. *Historical Statistics of the United States, Colonial Times to 1970.* Washington, DC: Government Printing Office.

U. S. Bureau of the Census. 1980. *Statistical Abstract of the United States.* Washington, DC: Government Printing Office.

U. S. Bureau of the Census. 1984. *Occupation by Industry, 1980.* Washington, DC: Government Printing Office.

U. S. Bureau of the Census. 1990a. *Statistical Abstract of the United States.* Washington, DC: Government Printing Office.

U. S. Bureau of the Census. 1990b. *Census of Retail Trade, 1987: Subject Series, Establishment and Firm Size.* Washington, DC: Government Printing Office.

U. S. Bureau of the Census. 1991. *Statistical Abstract of the United States.* Washington, DC: Government Printing Office.

U. S. Bureau of the Census. 1992. *Statistical Abstract of the United States.* Washington, DC: Government Printing Office.

U. S. Bureau of the Census. 1993. *Statistical Abstract of the United States.* Washington, DC: Government Printing Office.

U. S. Department of Commerce. 1980. *Current Developments in U. S. International Service Industries.* Washington, DC: International Trade Administration.

U. S. Department of Commerce. 1988. *Franchising in the Economy, 1986-1988.* Washington, DC: Government Printing Office.

United Nations Center on Transnational Corporations. 1983. *Transnational Corporations in World Development.* New York: United Nations.

Urquhart, Michael. 1984. "The Employment Shift to Services: Where Did It Come From?" *Monthly Labor Review* 107:15-22.

Useem, Michael. 1985. "The Rise of the Political Manager." *Sloan Management Review* 27:15-26.

Useem, Michael. 1986. *The Inner Circle: Large Corporations and the Rise of Business Activity in the U.S. and U.K.* New York: Oxford University Press.

Useem, Michael. 1990. "Business and Politics in the United States and the United Kingdom." Pp. 263-291 in *Structures of Capital*, edited by Sharon Zukin and Paul DiMaggio. Cambridge: Cambridge University Press.

Useem, Michael. 1993. *Executive Defense: Shareholder Power and Corporate Reorganization.* Cambridge, MA: Harvard University Press.

Vaupel, James W. and Joan P. Curhan. 1969. *The Making of Multinational Enterprise.* Boston: Division of Research, Graduate School of Business Administration.

Walker, Jack. 1983. "The Origins and Maintenance of Interest Groups in America." *American Political Science Review* 77:390-406.

Wallerstein, Immanuel. 1979. *The Capitalist World Economy*. Cambridge: Cambridge University Press.

Wallerstein, Immanuel. 1984. "Patterns and Perspectives of the Capitalist World Economy." *Contemporary Marxism* 9:59-70.

Wallerstein, Immanuel. 1986. "The United States and the World Crisis." Pp. 17-23 in *America's Changing Role in the World System*, edited by Terry Boswell and Albert Bergeson. London: Longman.

Walton, John. 1987. "Theory and Research on Industrialization." *Annual Review of Sociology* 13:89-108.

Weber, Max. 1981. *General Economic History*. New Brunswick: Transaction.

Weisbrod, Burton and Mark Schlesinger. 1986. "Nonprofit Ownership and the Response to Asymmetric Information: The Case of Nursing Homes." Pp. 133-51 in *The Economics of Nonprofit Institutions*, edited by Susan Rose-Ackerman. New York: Oxford University Press.

Whalley, Peter. 1990. "Markets, Managers, and Technical Autonomy in British Plants." Pp. 373-94 in *Structures of Capital*, edited by Sharon Zukin and Paul DiMaggio. Cambridge: Cambridge University Press.

White, Roderick. 1986. "Generic Business Strategies, Organizational Context, and Performance: An Empirical Investigation." *Strategic Management Journal* 7:217-31.

Williams, Rosalind H. 1982. *Dream Worlds: Mass Consumption in Late Nineteenth Century France*. Berkeley: University of California Press.

Williamson, Jeffrey and Peter Lindert. 1980. *American Inequality: A Macroeconomic History*. New York: Academic Press.

Williamson, Oliver. 1975. *Markets and Hierarchies*. New York: Free Press.

Williamson, Oliver. 1981. "The Economics of Organization." *American Journal of Sociology* 87:548-77.

Wilson, William. 1987. *The Truly Disadvantaged: The Inner City, The Underclass, and Public Policy*. Chicago: University of Chicago Press.

Wolfe, Alan. 1977. *The Limits of Legitimacy: Political Contradictions of Contemporary Capitalism*. New York: Basic Books.

Wolfe, Alan. 1987. "Toward a Political Sociology of Reaganism." *Contemporary Sociology* 16:31-3.

Wolfe, Alan. 1989. *Whose Keeper: Social Science and Moral Obligation*. Berkeley: University of California Press.

Wolff, Edward. 1992. "Changing Inequality of Wealth." *American Economic Review* 82:553-58.

Wolff, Edward and Marcia Marley. 1989. "Long-Term Trends in U.S. Wealth Inequality: Methodological Issues and Results." Pp. 765-839 in *The Measurement of Saving, Investment, and Wealth*, edited by Robert Lipsey and Helen Tice. Chicago: University of Chicago Press.

Wood, Adrian. 1994. *North-South Trade, Employment, and Inequality: Changing Fortunes in a Skill-Driven World*. Oxford: Clarendon Press.

World Bank. 1993. *World Tables, 1993*. Baltimore: The Johns Hopkins University Press.

Wright, Erik O. 1985. *Classes*. London: Verso.

Wright, Erik O. and Bill Martin. 1987. "The Transformation of the American Class Structure, 1960-1980." *American Journal of Sociology* 93:1-29.

Wright, Gavin. 1990. "The Origins of American Industrial Success, 1879-1940." *American Economic Review* 80:651-68.

Yip, George, Pierre Loewe, and Michael Yoshino. 1988. "How to Take Your Company to the Global Market." *Columbia Journal of World Business* 23:37-48.

Yoffie, David. 1987. "Corporate Strategies for Political Action: A Rational Model." Pp. 43-60 in *Business Strategy and Public Policy*, edited by Alfred Marcus, Allen Kaufman, and David Beam. New York: Quorum Books.

Zukin, Sharon and Paul DiMaggio. 1990. "Introduction." Pp. 1-36 in *Structures of Capital*, edited by Sharon Zukin and Paul DiMaggio. Cambridge: Cambridge University Press.

Index

About the Author

Joel I. Nelson is Professor of Sociology at the University of Minnesota. He has written extensively on stratification and the service economy. His interests center on the confluence of capitalism and industrial change. His publications include *Economic Inequality: Conflict Without Change, Sociological Analysis,* and numerous articles in journals including the *American Sociological Review,* the *American Journal of Sociology, Social Forces, Social Problems,* and *Research in Stratification and Mobility.* He has previously taught at the Université Paul Valery (Montpellier, France), where he was a Fulbright Fellow, and, most recently, Nankai University (Tianjin, People's Republic of China). He received his B.A. from Columbia College and his Ph.D. from Yale University.

Printed in the United Kingdom
by Lightning Source UK Ltd.
2330